unlet
Sorbovane 2001

Introducing
Democracy

Introducing Democracy

80 Questions and Answers

DAVID BEETHAM and KEVIN BOYLE

with cartoons by PLANTU

Polity Press   UNESCO Publishing

The right of David Beetham and Kevin Boyle to be identified as authors of this work has been asserted in accordance with the Copyright, Designs and Patents Act 1988.

First published in 1995 by Polity Press in association with Blackwell Publishers Ltd.

Editorial office:
Polity Press
65 Bridge Street
Cambridge CB2 1UR, UK

Marketing and production:
Blackwell Publishers Ltd
108 Cowley Road
Oxford OX4 1JF, UK

Blackwell Publishers Inc.
238 Main Street
Cambridge, MA 02142, USA

Distributors in the
United States of America

UNIPUB
4611-F Assembly Drive
Lanham, MD20706-4391
USA

United Nations Educational,
Scientific and Cultural Organization
7 Place de Fontenoy
75352 Paris
France

Library of Congress Cataloguing-in-Publication Data
Beetham, David.
   Introducing democracy : 80 questions and answers / David Beetham and Kevin Boyle.
      p.   cm.
   Includes bibliographical references.
   ISBN 0-7456-1519-8 (hbk.). —ISBN 0-7456-1520-1 (pbk.)
   1. Democracy—Miscellanea.   I. Boyle, Kevin.   II. Title.
JC423.B33   1995   95–22496
321.8—dc20   CIP

ISBN (UNESCO) 92-3-103081-7 (pbk)

A CIP catalogue record for this book is available from the British Library.

Typeset in 10 on 12 pt Bembo by CentraCet Limited, Cambridge
Printed in Great Britain by TJ Press Ltd, Padstow, Cornwall
This book is printed on acid-free paper.

This work was commissioned by UNESCO as part of its programme of education in democracy and human rights. It is appearing simultaneously in many languages.

The designations employed and the presentation of material throughout this publication do not imply the expression of any opinion whatsoever on the part of the UNESCO Secretariat concerning the legal status of any country, territory, city or area or of its authorities, or the delimitation of its frontiers or boundaries.

The authors are responsible for the choice and the presentation of the facts contained in this book and for the opinions expressed therein, which are not necessarily those of UNESCO and do not commit the Organization.

Universal Declaration of Human Rights

ARTICLE 21

1 Everyone has the right to take part in the government of his country, directly or through freely chosen representatives.
2 Everyone has the right of equal access to public service in his country.
3 The will of the people shall be the basis of the authority of government; this will shall be expressed in periodic and genuine elections which shall be by universal and equal suffrage and shall be held by secret vote or by equivalent free voting procedures.

Note: in the above Declaration 'his' is intended to include 'his or her', which is how it would be expressed today.

Contents

Contents

Contents

Authors' Preface

People often talk about 'democracy', but the word tends to mean different things to different people, and there is a good deal of confusion about what democracy actually involves. Is it individual freedom, multi-partyism, majority rule, minority rights, or what? Are there any agreed criteria by which we can judge a particular country democratic, or by which we may assess its progress in democracy? Are there set institutions or practices that a country must have for it to count as democratic, or can democracy be realized through many different means and in many different forms?

These are the kinds of question we seek to answer in this book. Some of our answers are more definitive than others. It should be evident that a country which has no competitive elections or universal suffrage, or where elected politicians have no effective control over the non-elected state officials, or where there are no guaranteed rights of association, assembly or free expression, cannot count as democratic. In some of these areas there exist recognized international standards to serve as our reference point, for example in respect of the protection of civil and political rights, or the integrity of election procedures, which have been evolved over many years by international bodies and NGOs in their monitoring of practice in particular countries. In other areas standards are much less well developed and less agreed. In yet others, countries will have a diversity of practices, none of which are more obviously democratic than others, for example in relation to their electoral systems, their head of government (president or prime minister), their legal systems, and so on. Understanding democracy is about understanding the legitimate diversity of democratic practice as well as what is essential to it.

In the post Cold War world, democracy has become a universal ideal, which almost all countries now aspire to. A book that explains what democracy involves is therefore particularly timely. It is addressed, first, to all those in the new and developing democracies – citizens, elected representatives, public servants – who want a clear reference book that offers straightforward answers to difficult questions about the practice of democracy. It is also addressed, secondly, to the many citizens of the developed democracies who are unclear about the democratic process in their own countries. For democracy to be maintained and deepened requires, above all, informed citizens. We hope that this volume will help that process of information or education.

We do not pretend that democracy today is without difficulty. Democracies face considerable challenges: from ethnic, religious and other divisions; from unemployment and economic recession or upheaval; from the loss of power to international institutions and processes; from a widespread feeling among people of powerlessness over their own lives. Although we offer no solutions to these problems, we do recognize their importance for the survival of democracy in the contemporary world.

But why should we value democracy in the first place? Perhaps now is the time for you, the reader, to find the answer for yourself in the pages that follow. The authors would welcome any comments you may have on the book, if you wish to write to us (c/o Polity Press). We hope you find it useful!

David Beetham
Kevin Boyle

1 | Basic Concepts and Principles

1 What is democracy?

Throughout our lives we are members of different groups or associations, from families, neighbourhoods, clubs and work-units to nations and states. In all such associations, from the smallest to the largest, decisions have to be taken for the association as a whole: about the goals to be pursued, about the rules to be followed, about the distribution of responsibilities and benefits between members. These can be called *collective* decisions, in contrast to *individual* decisions taken by people on behalf of themselves alone. Democracy belongs to this sphere of collective decision-making. It embodies the ideal that such decisions, affecting an association as a whole, should be taken by all its members, and that they should each have equal rights to take part in such decisions. Democracy, in other words, entails the twin principles of *popular control* over collective decision-making and *equality of rights* in the exercise of that control. To the extent that these principles are realized in the decision-making of any association, we can call it democratic.

1

Democracy in society and state

Defining democracy in this way makes two things clear at the outset. The first is that democracy does not just belong to the sphere of the state or of government, as we usually tend to think of it. Democratic principles are relevant to collective decision-making in any kind of association. Indeed, there is an important relation between democracy at the level of the state and democracy in the other institutions of society. However, because the state is the most inclusive association, with the right to regulate the affairs of society as a whole, the ability to raise compulsory taxation and the power of life and death over its members, democracy at the level of the state is of crucial importance. It is with democratic government, therefore, that we shall be mostly concerned.

A relative concept

The second point about our definition is that democracy is not an all-or-nothing affair, which an association possesses either in full or not at all. It is rather a matter of degree; of the extent to which the principles of popular control and political equality are realized; of greater or lesser approximations towards the ideal of equal participation in collective decision-making. Conventionally we have come to call a state 'democratic' if its government is accountable to the people through competitive election to public office, where all adults have an equal right to vote and to stand for election, and where civil and political rights are legally guaranteed. However, no such state in practice realizes the two principles of popular control and political equality as fully as it might. To that extent the work of democratization is never ended; and democrats everywhere are involved in struggles to consolidate and extend the realization of democratic principles, whatever regime or political system they happen to live under.

2 Why should we value democracy?

There are many reasons why democracy should be valued.

Equality of citizenship

Democracy aims to treat all people equally. 'Everyone to count for one and none for more than one', wrote the English legal theorist Jeremy Bentham in his attack on the aristocratic view that some people's lives were intrinsically more valuable than others. The principle of equality requires not only that people's interests should be attended to equally by government policy, but also that their views should count equally. 'We give no special power to wealth,' spoke an Athenian in one of Euripides' plays; 'the poor man's voice commands equal authority.' Critics of democracy have always objected that the mass of people are too ignorant, too uneducated and too short-sighted to take any part in determining public policy. To this democrats answer that the people certainly need information and the time to make sense of it, but are perfectly capable of acting responsibly when required to do so. Just as we expect all adults to take responsibility for directing their own personal lives, so they are also capable of taking a share in decisions affecting the life of their society.

Meeting popular needs

Democratic government is more likely than other types of government to meet the needs of ordinary people. The more say people have in the direction of policy, the more likely it is to reflect their concerns and aspirations. 'The cobbler makes the shoe,' went the ancient Athenian saying, 'but only the wearer can tell where it pinches.' It is ordinary people who experience the effects of government policy in practice, and only if there are effective and consistent channels of influence

3

and pressure from below does government policy reflect this experience. However well intentioned the holders of public office may be, if they are immune from popular influence or control, their policies will be at best inappropriate to people's needs and at worst self-serving and corrupt.

Pluralism and compromise

Democracy relies upon open debate, persuasion and compromise. The democratic emphasis on debate assumes not only that there are differences of opinion and interest on most questions of policy, but that such differences have a right to be expressed and listened to. Democracy thus presupposes diversity and plurality within society as well as equality between citizens. And when such diversity finds expression, the democratic method of resolving differences is through discussion, through persuasion and compromise, rather than by forcible imposition or the simple assertion of power. Democracies have often been caricatured as mere 'talking shops'. However, their capacity for public debate should be seen as a virtue rather than a vice, since it is the best means for securing consent to policy, and is not necessarily inconsistent with decisive action.

Guaranteeing basic freedoms

Democracy guarantees basic freedoms. Open discussion, as the method for expressing and resolving societal differences, cannot take place without those freedoms that are enshrined in conventions of civil and political rights: the rights of free speech and expression, of association with others, of movement, of security for the person. Democracies can be relied on to protect these rights, since they are essential to their own mode of existence. At best such rights allow for the personal development of individuals and produce collective

4

decisions that are better for being tested against a variety of argument and evidence.

Societal renewal

Democracy allows for societal renewal. By providing for the routine and peaceful removal of policies and politicians that have failed or outlived their usefulness, democratic systems are able to ensure societal and generational renewal without the massive upheaval or governmental disruption that attends the removal of key personnel in non-democratic regimes.

3 Where did the idea of democracy come from?

The idea that ordinary people should be entitled to a say in the decisions that affect their lives is one that has emerged as an aspiration in many different historical societies. It achieved a classical institutional form in Athens in the fifth and fourth centuries BC. From the early fifth century onwards, when property qualifications for public office were removed, each Athenian citizen had an equal right to take part in person in discussions and votes in the assembly on the laws and policies of the community, and also to share in their administration through jury service and membership of the administrative council, which were recruited in rotation by lot. The example of this first working democracy has been a reference point and source of inspiration to democrats ever since. The fact that it coincided with a period of Athenian economic and naval supremacy, and with an enormous flourishing of creative arts and philosophical enquiry, put paid to the idea that giving ordinary people a say in their affairs would produce either a society of drab uniformity or irresponsible government, as the critics of democracy have often asserted.

5

Direct democracy

Athenian democracy was both more and less democratic than the democracies we know today. It was more democratic in that citizens took part in person in the main decisions of the society ('direct democracy'), whereas today's representative democracies are indirect, and citizens stand at least at one remove from the decision-making processes of government and parliament. For direct democracy to be possible requires a relatively small citizen body capable of being accommodated in a single place of assembly, and one with enough time free from other responsibilities to be able to grasp the evidence and arguments necessary to make an informed political decision. Neither requirement for direct democracy is met by the citizen bodies of today, though there is scope for their involvement in direct decision-making at national level in elections and referenda, and for more continuous participation in decision-making at very local levels.

Exclusive citizenship

Athenian democracy was less democratic than democracies of today, however, in that citizenship was restricted to free-born males; it excluded women, slaves and resident foreigners, these groups ensuring the continuity of the domestic and productive work necessary to enable the male citizens to engage in political activity. So the active participation of a direct democracy was only possible at all because the citizenship was restricted. 'The people' certainly ruled, but they did so from a position of privilege.

Modern exclusivity

It is worth recalling that similar restrictions on citizenship existed in most Western Parliamentary systems until well into the twentieth century. The principle made famous by the French Revolution that 'all political authority stems from the people' was not intended to include all the people. Thus it is only in this century that women and propertyless males have been granted the suffrage in most Western countries; and even today not all adult residents of a country are entitled to vote in its elections, however much they may contribute to its economy.

4 Can a representative system be really democratic?

The eighteenth-century political theorist Rousseau thought not. In a representative system, he argued, people are only free once every few years at election time; thereafter they revert to a position of subordination to their rulers which is no better than slavery. This is an extreme version of the characteristic left-wing or radical criticism that representative systems are not properly democratic, in contrast to the right-wing objection that they give people too much say.

Control through election

The simple response is that a representative system is the best system yet devised for securing popular control over government in circumstances where the citizen body is numbered in millions and has not the time to devote itself continuously to political affairs. The theory is that the people control the government by electing its head (president or prime minister) and by choosing the members of a legislature or parliament that can exercise continuous supervision over the government on the people's behalf, through its power to approve or reject legislation and taxation. This popular control is only effective, however, to the extent that elections are 'free and fair', that government is open, and that parliament has sufficient powers in practice to scrutinize and control its actions.

Public opinion

Although elections are the principal means by which people have a say in government policy in a representative system, they are not the only means. People can join associations to campaign for and against changes in legislation; they can become members of political parties; they can lobby their representatives in person. Governments in turn can be required to consult those affected by their policies or a selected cross-section of the electorate. In practice, few representative governments are immune to expressions of public opinion such as are regularly provided by opinion polls or through the press, radio and television. Yet all these channels of popular influence are ultimately dependent upon the effectiveness of the electoral process. Governments will only listen seriously to the people when there is a realistic possibility that they will be turned out of office if they do not.

Direct and indirect control

So popular control in a representative system is secured by the direct influence people exercise over the direction of government policy and personnel at elections, through the continuous supervision exercised over government by a representative assembly or parliament and by the organized expression of public opinion through a variety of channels, which governments have to take into account.

Political equality

What about the second democratic principle (see question 1), that of political equality? A representative system involves inequality at least in this respect, that it gives a small number of the population the right to take political decisions on behalf of the rest. Within these limits, however, political equality can be achieved to the extent that there is an effective equal right for all citizens to stand for public office, to campaign on public issues and to obtain redress in the event of maladministration; and that the electoral system gives equal value to each person's vote. In practice most representative democracies do not fully satisfy these criteria, since political equality is substantially qualified by systematic differences in the wealth, time, access and other resources possessed by different groups of the population. It is one of the tasks of democrats in a representative system to find ways to reduce the political impact of these differences, as well as to make more effective the various mechanisms of popular control over government.

5   What role do political parties play in a democracy?

In a large society people can exercise little public influence as individuals, but can in association with others. Political parties bring together those who share similar views and interests to campaign for political office and influence. They perform a number of different functions. For the *electorate* they help simplify the electoral choice by offering broad policy positions and programmes between which to choose. For *governments* they provide a reasonably stable following of political supporters to enable them to achieve their pro- grammes once elected. For the *more politically committed* they provide an opportunity for involvement in public affairs, a means of political education and a channel for influencing public policy.

Fair competition

In a free and fair electoral system, the success of political parties depends upon the degree of electoral support they can win and maintain. This means that they have to keep in touch with popular opinion when framing their programmes and selecting candidates for office. If they do not, they will lose out to other parties or enable new parties to emerge to fill the vacuum. Political parties thus constitute a pivotal mechanism through which popular concerns are made effective in government. They will only fulfil this role, however, to the extent that the electoral competition between them is conducted 'on a level playing field', and that some parties do not have access to government resources or means of communicating with the electorate which others are denied. In particular this requires that parties in government should be made to keep a clear separation between their government and party activities, and between the organizations appropriate to each.

Social division

If open electoral competition between political parties is an indispensable feature of representative democracies, it is also their Achilles' heel. Open competition for government office is socially and politically divisive, and the stakes for those involved are usually high. A condition for democracy's survival, therefore, is that the cost to the losing parties and their supporters of exclusion from office is not insupportable. In particular they must have confidence in their ability to fight another electoral contest more successfully, and that their rights to organize, to campaign and to criticize the government will continue unimpaired despite their defeat.

6 Why are the media important to democracy?

All governments, in every type of political system, seek to win for their policies the support or acquiescence of the population. And since a large population can only be reached through the means of mass communication – press, radio and television – these media play a central political role in contemporary societies. In a democracy, however, the media have important functions other than simply to provide a channel for government propaganda. These are to investigate government, to inform the public, to provide a forum for political debate and to act as a channel for public opinion to, and for popular pressure upon, the government.

Journalist as 'watchdog'

The investigative and informative functions of the media are necessary to combat every government's preference for secrecy, and to offset the sheer weight of its public relations machine. A government can only be held publicly accountable if people know what it is doing, and if they have an independent means of testing official claims about its policies. Whilst the media must not overstep the bounds of privacy, it is their task to impart information and a conception of the public interest, and it is the right of the public to receive them. Were it otherwise, the media would be unable to play their vital role of 'public watchdog'.

Public debate

Besides the task of imparting independent information, the media also provide a forum for public debate, through which ministers and other public figures can be interrogated in ways that are accessible to a mass audience and that allow for

11

contributions from ordinary citizens. In doing so they also provide a vehicle for the expression of public opinion to the government. In all these respects the media serve to complement and reinforce the scrutinizing and deliberative functions of parliament by engaging the population as a whole.

Independence of the media

However, the media can only perform these key democratic tasks if they are properly independent, and not dominated either by the government itself or by powerful private interests. The dominance of a government can be limited by making the publicly financed media accountable to an independent commission or to representatives of citizens' groups, and by allowing competition from privately financed media. The dominance of powerful private interests can be restrained by limiting concentrations of media ownership, and by other forms of regulation. None of these on their own, however, can guarantee that the media fulfil their democratic role impartially and effectively. Ultimately that depends upon the independence and professionalism of journalists, editors and producers and upon a widespread public acknowledgement of the vital contribution that the media make to the democratic process.

7 Why are representative democracies called liberal democracies?

There is first a historical reason. Most Western states became liberal before they became democratic. That is to say they achieved a liberal constitutional order before they granted universal suffrage or developed mass political parties. The most important features of such an order were: the subordination of government or executive to the laws approved by an elected parliament (the 'rule of law'); guaranteed rights of the individual to due legal process and to the freedoms of speech, assembly and movement; a judiciary with sufficient independence of both parliament and executive to act as guardians of the law and of these individual rights. Historically, the democracies in which the suffrage was extended and mass political parties developed without the prior consolidation of these liberal constitutional features proved very insecure.

The rule of law

This brings us to a second, practical reason why liberal constitutionalism and democracy belong together. A government in a modern state has enormous powers at its disposal. Whatever its popularity, if it is not kept subject to the law like everyone else, or if it is not required to seek approval for legislation from parliament according to established procedures, or if it does not respect the liberties of its citizens, however unpopular on occasion their exercise may be, then people will rapidly lose the capacity to control it. Democracy is not a system that gives the people whatever they demand at a given moment, or in the shortest possible time, but one that secures the conditions for their influence and control over their government on an ongoing basis. And among these conditions have proved to be the basic elements of liberal constitutionalism already outlined: the rule of law, the separation of powers between executive, legislature and judiciary, and the guarantee of individual rights and liberties.

Constitutionalism and democracy

As the term 'constitutionalism' implies, these features, together with all the other component elements of democracy, are best protected in a written constitution, in which the rights and duties of citizens, and of the different organs of state, are explicitly defined and publicly known. The special position of the constitution is recognized when public officials are required to swear loyalty to it above party or sectional interest, and by the fact that it requires special measures, such as qualified majorities or referenda, to alter it. Yet in practice a written constitution is only secure to the extent that an independent judiciary has the authority and determination to enforce it and that the public at large is vigilant in its defence.

8 Is liberal democracy the only possible form of democracy?

The twentieth century has witnessed a number of attempts to construct democracy at the level of the state without the liberal inheritance, usually in single-party regimes. The most widespread have been communist systems. Here the argument for the single party was to prevent any reversal in the popular gains of the revolution and to eliminate the influence of private wealth and sectional interests on the political process. The ruling party was intended both as a channel for popular opinion from below and an instrument for mobilizing the population from above in support of government policy.

Loss of accountability

There was undoubtedly a certain democratic impetus behind all this, though it is unfashionable now to say so. However, the absence of any freedom of speech and association meant that only those views could be expressed, and only those organizations established, that were approved by the party hierarchy; and hence that the influence of citizens over policy and the accountability of public officials to them were severely limited. Despite considerable economic achievements, communist systems have been characterized by

authoritarian rule, widespread repression and illegality, and have only been able to maintain themselves through the substantial apparatus of a police state.

Single-party rule

A similar, if less extreme, fate has met the African attempts to construct single-party democracies on non-communist lines. Here again the intentions were laudable. A single party would prevent the divisiveness of multi-party competition, it was argued, especially in ethnically divided societies, and would reflect the traditional emphasis on consensus, to which the idea of a 'loyal opposition' was quite alien. Moreover, the voters would be given a choice between candidates at election time and the chance to remove unpopular ministers, though competition would not go beyond the party and its agreed programme. Once again, however, the inability of people to organize independently of the ruling party and to oppose it at elections meant that governments and their leaders became authoritarian and unresponsive, while the lack of any effective separation of powers meant that the rule of law, the protection of civil liberties and the accountability of the government to the public through parliament could not be guaranteed.

Liberalism and democracy

The only conclusion that can be drawn from these histories is that attempts to construct democracy without liberalism are doomed to failure. Whatever disadvantages the freedom of association and open electoral competition may have, they have proved indispensable means to ensure the continuity of popular influence and control over government, while the rule of law and the separation of powers have guaranteed the necessary procedural constraints upon government to make that control effective. Certainly there remains much room

17

for experimentation within the liberal–democratic framework and for adaptation to local conditions. But it is mistaken to imagine that democratic forms that work in small–scale contexts or in the framework of traditional society can without hazard be transposed to the level of the state. The modern state is a structure of enormous power, and the historical struggles of Western liberals and constitutionalists to subject the absolutist state of the early modern period to some degree of public control and accountability constitute an important lesson for contemporary democrats.

9 Is a free-market economy necessary to democracy?

This is a complex question to which there is no unequivocal answer. On one side a system of production and distribution based upon the principle of free exchange can be seen as conducive to democracy. Like democracy, the market treats individuals non-paternalistically, as the best judges of their own interests and as responsible for their own choices. It makes the consumer sovereign in much the same way as the voter is sovereign in a democracy, with the success of firms depending upon the degree to which customers support them, much as political parties depend upon the degree of electoral support they obtain. Moreover, the market sets limits to the power of the state by decentralizing economic decisions and by dispersing opportunity, information and resources within civil society. It prevents people from being beholden to the state for their economic destinies or for the financing of any independent political and cultural activity. In all these ways the market can be seen as supportive of democracy.

Disadvantages of the market

On the other side, however, the market, if left to itself, generates booms and slumps in production which cause enormous economic hardship and dislocation. It makes a country vulnerable to international fluctuations in prices and trade that deprive it of self-determination in its economic policy. Domestically, the market intensifies the differences of capacity and resources that various economic agents bring to it, in a way that compromises the political equality demanded by democracy. And it treats the labour of workers as just another commodity subject to the laws of supply and demand, to be dispensed with if unwanted, in a manner that is inconsistent with the value which the status of citizenship confers on the individual. It is hardly surprising, therefore, that the early industrializing countries of Western Europe found that the free market was incompatible with a democratic suffrage, which they resisted throughout most of the nineteenth century; or that many subsequent attempts to run a laissez-faire economy have required authoritarian governments to contain popular discontent. Since the Second World War Western governments have sought to reconcile democracy with a market economy by substantial market regulation and intervention, by economic redistribution and by creating a system of welfare rights to protect the most vulnerable from the market's vicissitudes.

Ambiguous relationship

Those attracted by the simplicities of laissez-faire would do well to note these ambiguities in the relation between democracy and the market. At the same time, the centrally planned economies of socialism required an uncontrollable bureaucratic apparatus to administer them, allowed the state to absorb all society's energy and initiative and created huge political inequalities and privileges, none of which were

19

compatible with democracy. Whether a decentralized system of socially owned enterprises within a market economy could prove either economically workable or consistent with a multi-party democracy remains an unresolved question. The only form of democratic socialism that has so far proved viable in practice has been the social democracy of the West and North European countries since 1945. And that has been more a modification of capitalism than its outright replacement.

10 Is decision by the majority always democratic?

It is a common misconception to equate democracy with majority rule. If we take the term democracy literally as rule by the people, then this means rule by the whole people, not by one part of the people over another. In other words, the crucial democratic feature is the rights of decision-making that all share equally, whereas decision by the majority is simply a procedural device for resolving disagreement when other methods (discussion, amendment, compromise) have been exhausted. Of course majority decision must be more democratic than allowing minorities to decide or to obstruct the will of the majority; but in so far as it leaves the minority impotent, without any influence on the outcome, it should be regarded more as a rough and ready device for reaching decisions than as the acme of democratic perfection.

Principle of reciprocity

Defenders of majority rule point out that those in the minority on one occasion may be in the majority on the next, and that their lack of influence in one decision, or in one election, will be compensated by 'winning' later. Minority consent to the majority view, in other words, rests upon a norm of reciprocity: their turn to be in the majority will come, and others will have to respect it in the same manner as they have done. However, this principle of reciprocity breaks down if the decision of the majority impairs a minority's capacity to canvass its views in the future; or if the minority is a 'permanent' one; or if the issue being decided is so vital to the minority that it cannot be compensated by winning on different issues in the future. Each of these cases requires separate examination.

Majority and individual rights

When the decision of a majority (or of a government acting with majority support) infringes the basic democratic rights of an individual or group, it must by definition be undemocratic. These basic rights are those necessary to enable people to contribute to political life: the freedoms of speech, movement and association; the right to vote and to stand for public office. The guarantee of these rights equally to all citizens constitutes the bedrock of a democratic system; ideally they should be given special protection in a constitution or bill of rights, where they remain immune from majority infringement. The difficult question of when they can be justifiably suspended or qualified *for everyone* will be discussed later (see questions 59–61).

Permanent minorities

The principle of reciprocity breaks down, secondly, where the minority is a 'permanent' one, defined by race, religion, language, ethnicity, or some other permanent characteristic. When the system of party competition coincides with these communities, rather than cuts across them, such a minority may be permanently excluded from governmental office and from all prospect of political influence. Various constitutional devices are available to prevent a condition of permanent

21

subordination for such a minority: a system of power-sharing, whereby they are accorded positions in the government and other public offices proportionate to their numbers; the right to veto legislation which threatens their vital interests; substantial autonomy in the running of their own affairs. Which of these devices is most appropriate will depend upon the circumstances. Whatever the device, however, the right of a people to practise their own culture is now recognized as a basic human right, which requires constitutional protection (see question 63).

Intense minorities

Finally, there is the 'intense' minority. A group may feel that a particular issue is so important that impotence in the face of the majority can never be compensated by its being part of a majority on other occasions or on other issues. Such situations simply cannot be legislated for. But a wise majority will go some way towards meeting the minority, if at all possible, rather than use its majority position simply to overrule them. Democracy is only sustainable if people can agree to continue living together. And that requires that majorities and the governments representing them should be prepared to exercise a measure of self-restraint, and do not always use the majority procedure to capture everything for themselves and their own point of view.

11 Can an individual legitimately disobey the law in a democracy?

Civil disobedience – the public and non-violent breaking of the law in defence of some important principle or vital interest – has an honourable place in the history of democracy. It is to be distinguished from criminal law-breaking by its openness, by its political purpose and by the fact that those involved do not seek to evade prosecution or punishment for their offences. Its aim is usually to draw attention to some injustice or outrage perpetrated by public authorities or powerful private bodies, and to compel a rethink of the relevant policy, when other methods of publicity and persuasion have proved ineffective. Less usually, it seeks to make the offending policy unworkable through the organization of mass resistance. However, because it breaks the principle of reciprocity on which consent to the law in a democracy is based (see question 10), it should only be contemplated in exceptional circumstances, and only then as a last resort.

Integrity of the law

Critics of civil disobedience argue that breaking the law can never be justified. The law is the foundation of a civilized society, and disregard for it by one person of group only encourages others to act likewise. If everyone were to pick and choose which laws they were to obey, the framework of law on which we all depend would rapidly disintegrate. Moreover, in a democratic society people have constitutional channels open to them through which to change the law: voting in elections, lobbying representatives, legal campaigning to persuade citizens and the government of the need to change the offending law or policy. And the very act of taking part in an election indicates consent to the outcome and agreement to abide by the policies the winning side has campaigned upon. Civil disobedience is thus an affront to democracy as well as to the rule of law.

Law and justice

Defenders of the right to civil disobedience point out that consent to abide by the outcome of an election cannot commit a person to obey every law or cooperate with every policy of the government however unjust it may be. Sometimes the

23

constitutional channels of campaign and protest may simply take too long, while the damage being done is irreversible. In practice the voices of ordinary people tend to be drowned by the propaganda of governments and powerful vested interests. In these respects civil disobedience can serve as a contribution to democracy, rather than its antithesis, by bringing opposition dramatically to public attention. In any case the final court of decision about right and wrong must be the individual conscience, and no one can evade responsibility for the persistence of unjust laws simply by doing nothing. The historical record suggests that more damage is done by passive acquiescence in the face of oppressive laws than by principled disobedience.

Individual conscience

These differences of view cannot be easily resolved by appeal to general considerations. Much depends upon the precise circumstances of each case, upon the balance between the conflicting principles involved and upon an assessment of their respective consequences. Ultimately the issue can only be resolved by each individual for him- or herself. One area where the importance of individual conscience is now officially recognized is the right of conscientious objection to military service; and many states, in making room for alternative forms of service, are acknowledging the moral force of such objection.

12 Is there any connection between nationalism and democracy?

It is often claimed that nationalism and democracy are the chief competing ideologies of the contemporary world.

What this claim overlooks is that they share a common historical and ideological origin in the principle of the French Revolution that all political authority stems from the people. The nationalist belief in the self-determination of peoples, each within its own state, is closely akin to the democratic principle that the people of a country should be self-determining in their own affairs. If the people are to rule, then who constitutes the people becomes a pressing political question.

Nationalism and exclusivity

However, this is not the end of the matter. Whereas democracy is a universalistic doctrine, emphasizing the common human capacity for self-determination, which all share despite their differences, nationalism is particularistic, emphasizing the differences between peoples, and the value of a nation's distinctive culture, tradition and ways of living. Nationalism tends to be exclusive whereas democracy is inclusive. And this exclusivity becomes profoundly undemocratic when it leads to the denial of citizenship rights to settled residents of a territory simply because they do not share the language, religion or ethnic origins of the most numerous national group. If all states coincided neatly with a single homogeneous people or nation there would be no problem. In practice, however, centuries of migration and conquest have so intermingled the peoples of the world that the concept of the nation-state as the home of a single national or ethnic grouping is nowhere to be realized.

Nationalism and democratic rights

Although national demands for self-determination can therefore be seen as consistent with democratic principle, the denial of equal political rights to settled residents or the refusal to grant any autonomy to minority peoples within a territory must be judged undemocratic. Moreover, in view of the manifest potential of such denials to disrupt the peace, both within and between states, they cannot simply be regarded as an internal matter, to be decided by the country in question. Basic democratic rights, as a part of human rights, are now regarded as a common property and legitimate aspiration of all mankind, and their denial a proper ground for concern and even, where appropriate, for sanction on the part of the international community. The particularism of nationhood and ethnicity, in other words, can now only be legitimately asserted on the basis of acknowledging our common humanity, and not at its expense.

13 Can any country attain democratic government?

The nineteenth-century liberal philosopher J. S. Mill argued that democratic government required an advanced level of civilization. Non-Western countries were incapable of self-government, he believed, and required a benevolent despotism to rule them, preferably administered by the West. This racist judgement was characteristic of even the most enlightened thinkers of the period. Although having an educated population is certainly advantageous for a democracy, because it diminishes the gulf between rulers and ruled, there is no evidence that the lack of a formal education renders people incapable of understanding and discussing the issues that affect them, or of taking responsibility for their own affairs. And the track record of despotism, whether imperial or domestic, is anything but benevolent.

Popular struggle

The historical record indicates that democracy is rarely established without widespread popular struggle and mobilization, sometimes over a lengthy period and at considerable personal cost. Ordinary people have to be convinced of the necessity of democratic government to the realization of their basic aspirations, and must organize to demand it. In other words, democracy does not come handed down from above. Traditional rulers, military dictators, communist *apparatchiks*, life presidents, foreign occupiers – none of them give up power voluntarily, but only when their regimes have become widely discredited, and popular mobilization has convinced them that their continuation in power can only provoke deepening disorder and ungovernability.

International support

Support from democracies abroad can certainly assist in victory for democratic forces and the attainment of a democratic constitution. During the Cold War, however, Western democracies were interested more in limiting the spread of communism in other countries than in encouraging democracy, and to this end they helped sustain some highly undemocratic regimes in power. Since the end of the Cold War the balance of international activity has shifted decisively towards supporting democratic movements and governments. Although such support is important, it can be no substitute for a people's own struggle against authoritarian rule. After all, there is something self-contradictory about a country's having self-government imposed upon it from outside; and in any case such a regime is unlikely to last for long.

14 Once achieved, how can democracy be maintained?

There is no simple recipe. The Western democracies only achieved stability over a long period, and after experiencing periodic reversals at the hands of aristocratic reaction, military dictatorship or fascism. Circumstances may simply prove too unfavourable for democratic sustainability in some of the recently established democracies. Thus social divisions may run too deep to be accommodated within a free political order. Or the economy may be too impoverished to enable legitimate popular expectations to be met. Or the military may be too powerful and too unreconciled to a non-political role.

Democratic consolidation

However, it is mistaken to imagine that people are powerless in the face of unfavourable conditions. Measures can be taken to consolidate democratic institutions so as to withstand the pressures to which they will inevitably be subject. Much depends, for example, on the quality and training of the professionals who occupy key positions within the state: the judiciary and constitutional lawyers, parliamentary clerks, election officers and the civil service more widely. Political parties need to be built up and to have access to training for their own cadres. The principal institutions of civil society – the media, businesses, trade unions, non-governmental organizations in general (NGOs) – need to develop the capacity to act independently of the state and its tutelage. Much also depends upon the ability and integrity of senior political leaders and upon their commitment to democratic and constitutional politics, as well as to the solution of immediate problems and the continuation of their own power.

Two-sided struggle

The maintenance of democracy can perhaps best be seen as a campaign waged on two fronts simultaneously. On one side is the struggle against anti-democratic forces, which may never have reconciled themselves to free institutions or to the influence of ordinary people on the political process. On the other side is the struggle to contain the divisive features of democratic politics itself, such as the competition for government office and the temptation to treat politics as a game in which the winners take all the prizes. The first struggle will depend upon the breadth of the institutions and groups within society that have an interest in the survival of democracy and a readiness to defend it. The second will depend upon a certain self-restraint in the exercise of power and a willingness to keep open the dialogue with political opponents, as well as upon respect by the population at large for the political rights of others.

15 What are the chief components of a functioning democracy?

There are four main components or building blocks of a functioning democracy. These are: free and fair elections; open and accountable government; civil and political rights; a democratic or 'civil' society. These components have been touched on in answers to previous questions; here they will be described more systematically, since they provide the framework for the following sets of questions. This framework can be represented diagrammatically as a 'democratic pyramid', in which each component is necessary to the whole (see figure 1).

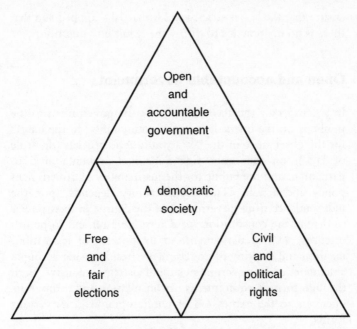

Figure 1   The democratic pyramid

Free and fair elections

Competitive elections are the main device whereby public officials are rendered accountable and subject to popular control. They also constitute an important arena for ensuring political equality between citizens, both in access to public office and in the value of their votes. The criterion of 'free and fair elections' embraces in the first place the electoral *system*, i.e. the laws governing which offices are electable, who may stand for them, when elections are to be held, who may vote, how constituencies are to be defined, how votes are to be aggregated to select the winners, and so on. Second is the electoral *process*, i.e. how individual elections are conducted in practice, from the initial registration of voters, through the campaign, to the counting of the ballots, to

31

ensure that the law is strictly and impartially applied and that there is no malpractice to throw the result into question.

Open and accountable government

In a democracy the accountability of the government to the public is on the one side a *legal* accountability: to the courts for the observance of the law by all public officials (the 'rule of law'); on the other side a *political* accountability: to parliament and the public for the justifiability of government policy and actions. This accountability depends upon the independence from government of the courts, in their power to defend the constitution, to determine guilt and to punish offences, and of parliament, in its powers of legislation, taxation and scrutiny of government. Besides being accountable, democratic government should also be responsive, both through formal requirements of consultation and through its openness to the expression of public opinion in its various forms.

Civil and political rights

Civil and political rights encompass those freedoms – of expression, association, movement, and so on – which are a necessary condition for people to act politically, whether in terms of self-organization within civil society or to bring influence to bear upon government. Although these rights are properly guaranteed to *individuals*, as a part of human rights more generally, their value lies in the context of *collective* action: joining with others for common ends, campaigning, influencing public opinion, etc. It is thus mistaken to see individual rights as necessarily antithetical to collective purposes, or to the processes of collective decision-making and their popular control, for which they constitute rather the necessary foundation.

A democratic or 'civil' society

The idea of a 'civil' society indicates that democracy needs to have social associations of all kinds that are organized *independently* of the state. Only in this way can the power of the state be limited, can public opinion be articulated from below rather than managed from above, and can society achieve the self-confidence to resist arbitrary rule. The principle that such associations should be not only independent but also *internally democratic* embodies the idea that democracy at the level of the state will only be weakly rooted if the rest of society is run on autocratic lines. If people are conditioned to authoritarianism in the family, the school and the church, and if they have no experience of self-organization or co-determination in the workplace, the neighbourhood and voluntary associations, they are unlikely to be active citizens or feel any responsibility for the condition of their society at large.

2 | Free and Fair Elections

16 Why are elections important?

The purpose of elections at national level is twofold. First is to choose the head of government or chief executive and the broad policy that the government will pursue. Second is to choose the members of the representative assembly, legislature or parliament, who will decide on legislation and taxation and scrutinize the work of the government on the people's behalf. In a *presidential* system, where the president is head of the government, these two purposes are clearly distinguished by having separate elections for president and members of the legislature; such elections may or may not take place at the same time. In a *prime-ministerial* or *parliamentary* system, one set of elections will fulfil both purposes, since it is the elected members of parliament who will determine the head of the government on the basis of which party leader can win majority support in parliament.

Elections and popular control

The regular election of these public officials in an open and competitive process constitutes the chief instrument of popular control in a representative democracy. Elections demonstrate that political power derives from the people and is held

34

in trust for them; and that it is to the people that politicians must account for their actions. In the last resort only the possibility of being turned out of office ensures that those elected fulfil their trust and maintain the standards of public office, and guarantees those changes in the personnel and policies of government that changing circumstances require.

17 Should the Head of State be popularly elected?

The office of Head of State should be a largely ceremonial and symbolic one, representing the unity of the nation above the competition of party, the continuity of the state above the changeability of governments, the permanence of the constitution above the temporality of particular legislation. This symbolic function can attain a special importance at moments of national crisis or constitutional controversy, when the Head of State may come to exercise considerable discretionary power.

Different systems

In a presidential system, the elected president combines the ceremonial function of Head of State with the executive function of head of government (as in Russia, the USA and most Latin American countries). In a parliamentary republic, the Head of State will be a non-executive president, elected either directly or by parliament (as in Germany, Ireland, India, etc.). In a constitutional monarchy, the Head of State will be determined by heredity and will hold office for life (as in Belgium, Spain, the UK).

No best one

Which of these is best? There is no simple answer, as each has to be assessed in the context of a constitutional system as a whole. The executive presidency has the disadvantage that the Head of State is not isolated from the controversy of day-to-day politics or the odium of unpopular or failed policies. On the other hand, a non-elected monarchy is hardly a democratic institution, especially where it constitutes the apex of a system of landed wealth and aristocratic status. At the very least, a monarchy should have been subject to approval by popular referendum, and its prerogatives should be carefully delimited by a written constitution.

18 What other public offices should be popularly elected?

Since the elected chief executive is responsible to the public and to parliament for the conduct and competence of all civil servants in the employ of a national government, there is a strong argument for making such posts subject to appointment from above rather than election from below, provided the initial recruitment to them is open to any qualified member of society. However, a democracy also requires public services that are responsive to *local* needs and to the variability of local circumstances. Here lies the justification for having elected bodies to supervise the administration of local services – health, education, the police, and so on – and to take responsibility for local government in general.

Elections and the judiciary

Should the judiciary be elected? At first sight consistency would seem to require that, just as the legislature and chief executive are popularly elected, so should the judiciary be. However, since the judiciary serves a legal rather than a political function, whose virtue lies in consistency and impartiality rather than popularity, the tenure of office should be immune from popular disapproval or the danger of becoming too closely identified with a particular section of the community. It is the task of parliament to ensure that legislation, the levels of sentence, etc., remain in touch with public opinion, not that of the judiciary itself. At the same time the pattern of recruitment to the judiciary is a matter of legitimate democratic concern, especially where it works to disadvantage substantial sections of society, such as women or members of ethnic or other minorities. (Judicial appointments are discussed in question 40.)

19 Should there be more than one elected chamber of parliament?

The argument for having a second chamber of parliament, elected on a basis different from the first, rests on the desirability of ensuring the fullest consideration of and the widest support for legislation. It is particularly important in a federal system, where the second chamber represents the interests of the member states rather than of the territory considered as a whole. It can also act as a useful check on legislation in states without any constitutional guarantee of individual rights.

Different elections

Methods of election will normally differ between the two chambers, the upper one being elected indirectly, or on the basis of different constituencies, or over a different timescale so that, say, only some members come up for election at any one time. In a parliamentary system, the simultaneous direct

37

election of the lower chamber by the country as a whole makes it the chief source of popular legitimacy for the government, and gives it the priority in legislation; at most the upper chamber will have a limited delaying or veto power. There is nothing whatsoever to be said for the survival in a democracy of a second chamber that is unelected.

20 How frequently should elections take place?

The demand of radical democrats in nineteenth-century Europe was for annual elections to parliament, in order to keep effective control over representatives. However, the business of modern government and parliament requires a longer period than one year for the effective management of an economy, and for the consequences of policies to work through. A four-year cycle is now usually accepted as a reasonable compromise between a government's need for continuity on the one hand and the requirements of responsiveness and accountability on the other.

Timing of elections

Whatever the precise duration of the elected offices, however, it is important that the timing of an election should not rest with the government in power. As will be discussed below (see question 31), it is a cardinal principle of 'free and fair' elections that the electoral process should not be controlled by or give an unfair advantage to the party or parties in office. This requirement should extend to the timing, as well as the conduct, of elections.

21 Should anyone be excluded from the right to vote?

The usual exclusions operating in most democracies are children, criminals and foreign residents. This is a very mixed bag, and different reasons clearly apply for each category. The exclusion of children below a certain age is justified by both common sense and developmental psychology. Below a certain age most children do not have sufficient experience or sufficient sense of the longer-term consequences of their choices to be treated non-paternalistically. In most societies there is a clustering of rights which children attain together and which define adulthood: the right to marry, to own property, to initiate legal proceedings in one's own person and to vote. These usually coincide around the age of eighteen, with the latest age for leaving secondary school and the obligation for military service.

Determinate age limit

Any fixed age, however, is bound to be somewhat arbitrary. There is evidence that children nowadays mature earlier than in the past. Some rights, for example to earn wages in full-time employment, they attain before eighteen. And there is regrettable truth in the argument that some children need protection *from* the adults who are responsible for them, and that this requires that they be given a say in their lives much earlier. In any case, maturing is a continuous process, and preparation for democratic citizenship should involve some participation in collective decision-making in family and school from the earliest age possible. However, none of these considerations is sufficiently compelling to merit reducing the voting age in public elections significantly below eighteen, or to undermine the symbolic importance of having a particular moment when everyone is recognized by society as attaining the status and rights of adulthood together.

Criminals and the vote

The argument for debarring criminals serving prison sentences from the vote is that those found guilty of serious offences against the law have forfeited the right to any say in framing it. On the other side, though, it can be argued that the loss of freedom should not entail the loss of all other rights of citizenship; and that prisoners particularly require access to elected representatives to help protect them against illegal or inhumane treatment and conditions.

Resident aliens

Finally, and most contentiously, there is the exclusion of resident aliens. Here the right to vote involves a larger issue: the qualifications for access to citizenship. If we acknowledge that democracy emerged from the eighteenth-century challenge to the dynastic principle that birth or inheritance was the exclusive basis for political rights, then we cannot with consistency make it the sole criterion of citizenship to the exclusion of legally settled residence in a country. How long counts as 'settled' may be a matter of dispute, but five years would be reasonable.

22 What should be the procedures for voter registration?

Voter registration sounds like a technical matter, but in practice the procedures adopted have a considerable significance for the right to vote. The point of having a register of electors compiled before an election takes place is simple: voters have to be identified in person and their act of voting recorded so that no one votes twice, impersonates another voter or otherwise votes without being entitled to do so.

However, there are various ways in which the procedures for registration may discourage citizens from registering their entitlement or from exercising it in practice. Registration may be voluntary and may depend upon the unpaid efforts of party volunteers. It may take place so long before an election that it is already well out of date when the election is called. Or the register may be used for other state purposes, such as a record of taxation, marital or occupational status, which citizens should properly be required to declare separately. The procedure which accords with best democratic practice is that registration should be compulsory, that the compilation of the register should be carried out by paid officials trained for the purpose, and as near as practicable to an election, and that the register should be kept physically and organizationally separate from other state records.

23 Should voting be compulsory?

The argument for making voting compulsory (as, for example, it is in Australia) is that helping to choose a government and to elect representatives is a civic duty as well as a right, and one which past generations have struggled to achieve. The act of abstention should be positively recorded on the ballot paper, rather than simply expressed by non-attendance, along with the apathetic, the absent and the deceased. Against this it can be argued that there is something contradictory about making a 'free election' compulsory, or requiring people to exercise their 'rights'; and that the numbers of voters abstaining, and their incidence as between different groups of the population, constitute an important signal or early warning sign of inadequacies in the democratic process.

Compulsory registration

Most democracies favour the latter arguments and treat voting as voluntary. But is this inconsistent with making registration compulsory, as many also do? Not necessarily. It is a necessary precondition of choosing whether to exercise the vote or not that a person should be on the electoral register; and the register may also be used for legitimate electoral purposes, such as equalizing the number of voters between constituencies, which require a full and accurate return to be made.

24 Why should the ballot be secret?

The English liberal philosopher J. S. Mill believed that voting should be carried out in public, so that electors would be answerable to their fellow citizens for the way they cast their votes, and so be encouraged to consider the wider public interest rather than just their narrow private interest. Few later thinkers have endorsed this rather lofty view. In practice public voting renders electors vulnerable to improper pressure from the powerful – employers, landowners, priests, superiors of all kinds – and to systematic bribery from those seeking election. The secret ballot is now established as a central feature of all democratic systems.

25 Who should be entitled to stand for office?

In principle anyone entitled to vote should also be entitled to stand for office. The practice in some countries of setting a higher age threshold for candidates than for electors seems unnecessary, given that no one is likely to be a credible

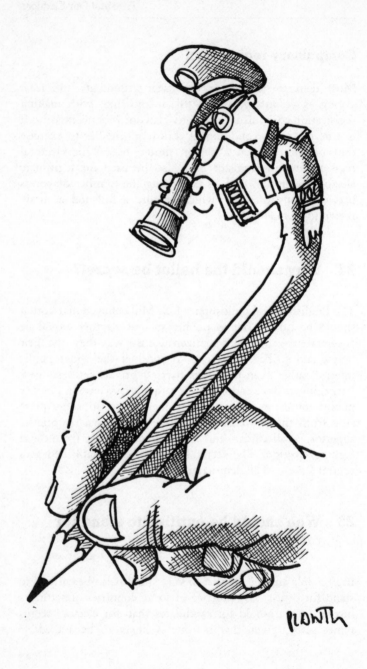

candidate for higher office who has not already acquired some experience in public affairs.

Conditions for nomination

A different question concerns the procedures for nomination or registering a candidacy. Most electoral systems seek to deter frivolous candidates by requiring a minimum number of supporting signatures from registered electors in the relevant constituency, and/or by requiring a monetary deposit, to be forfeited if a minimum number of votes is not obtained. The danger of both practices is that they may deter serious as well as frivolous candidates, especially where they represent new parties or political forces. In some countries only candidates representing previously registered parties may stand. Again this is designed to deter the frivolous, but it may also serve as a means of political control over parties and candidates and so limit the legitimate expression of electoral opinion.

Primary elections

In the USA the candidates for each party are chosen by a primary election restricted to the registered voters of the relevant party. Although this practice gives voters a say in who stands for office as well as who is elected to it, it enormously increases the cost of elections and creates a bias in favour of those who are personally rich or who have wealthy backers. In view of this drawback, it is more usual to have candidates chosen by balloting all party *members* in the relevant district or constituency, though even this degree of democracy in candidate selection is by no means universal.

26 Why are so few women elected to public office?

In Western democracies the proportion of representatives who are women is very low compared with the proportion of women in the electorates. The average for long-established democracies is under 15%, ranging from a mean of about 35% for the Nordic countries to about 10% for most of the rest, with a low of 6% for France. The reasons for this situation are partly historical, partly domestic and partly political. For most of human history women have been considered naturally unsuited to political activity, and have been formally or informally excluded from it, thus confirming the belief in their unsuitability. The legacy of these past beliefs, reinforced by the unequal domestic division of labour, whereby women continue to take the major responsibility for child-rearing and servicing the home, handicaps women in the pursuit of political office. Politics is an enormously time-consuming activity; the hours worked by the government and parliament are often highly unsocial; and the activity itself, which puts a premium on competition, party rivalry and personal aggrandizement, is one that women tend to find more uncongenial than men.

Why equality matters

Does this matter? From the standpoint of political equality it matters if any section of society is markedly privileged in its access to public office, whether elected or non-elected. There is also good reason to suppose that issues affecting women are not taken so seriously by men, or given sufficient priority in the competition for public funding. Although women do not by any means all have the same views and interests, there is something offensive to many women about a largely male parliament deciding legislation on contraception, abortion, rape, and so on. In any case, society as a whole is the poorer

46

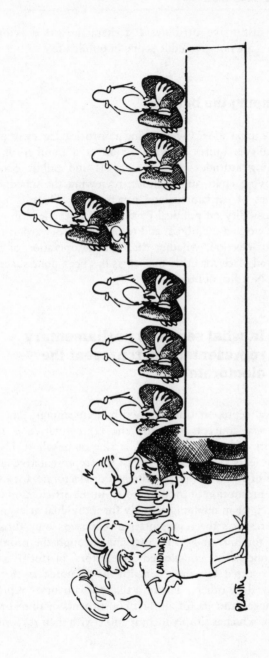

if the distinctive attributes and characteristics developed by women are not given due scope in public life.

Changing the balance

What can be done? Overcoming a historical legacy of political inequality requires relevant action at a number of levels: changing attitudes through schools and public education; improving child-care facilities; reviewing the schedules and facilities of parliament; and much more. There is a special responsibility on political parties to take the lead in encouraging women members, and to put them forward as candidates for election, whether through the operation of quotas, reserved places or other means, as has been done successfully in the Nordic countries.

27 In what sense do parliamentary representatives represent the electorate?

Political representation has two basic meanings. The first is an *agency* concept, whereby the representative is seen as 'authorized by', 'standing for', 'acting on behalf of' his or her constituents. In some respects the representative acts on behalf of *all* his or her constituents or electorate: for example in the promotion of local interests, in the articulation of local opinion, or in pursuing remedy for individual grievances. In other respects the representative represents only those who voted for him or her: by carrying through the programme and policies that constituted the electoral platform, and that were rejected by some constituents as much as they were approved by others. The idea that parliamentary representatives speak and act for all their constituents in all respects is a fiction, which is simply incompatible with their responsibility to act consistently with the programmes on which they were elected and to be accountable for their effective fulfilment.

Microcosmic representation

The second concept of political representation is a *microcosmic* one, and concerns the representative assembly as a whole, rather than individual representatives. A legislative assembly can be said to be representative to the extent that it reflects the character of the electorate at large in some relevant respect: its social composition, its geographical distribution, its votes for the different parties. Which of these respects is most important? All matter, but in a system in which the electoral choice is between national parties offering competing programmes of legislation, the requirement that the assembly's composition should reflect the national vote for the respective parties can be argued to be the most important. It is most fully met in proportional electoral systems (see question 28).

Two democratic principles

These two concepts of representation, the agential and the microcosmic, can be seen to embody the two basic principles of democracy already outlined in question 1. The principle of popular sovereignty – that all political authority stems from the people and that parliament and government should be subject to popular control – is encapsulated in the idea of the representative as *agent* of the electorate: authorized by, acting for, accountable to and removable by them. The second, *microcosmic*, conception of representation embraces the principle of political equality: each vote should have the same weight or value, regardless of where people happen to live or which party they vote for. To the extent that this principle is met, the assembly will be microcosmically representative of

the electorate, and reflect its geographical distribution and the distribution of the popular vote between the different parties.

28 What are the differences between different electoral systems?

There are numerous electoral systems in use throughout the world, but only the five main types will be outlined here. The merits of each will be considered in the answer to the next question; here they are simply described.

The plurality system

The plurality or 'first past the post' system is used for legislative elections in the USA, most of Latin America, also in the UK and many of its former colonies. Under this system the country is divided into single-member constituencies of roughly equal size. Voters may vote for only one candidate on the ballot paper, and the candidate who wins the most votes is elected, whether or not he or she wins a majority of the votes cast.

The alternative vote

The alternative vote is used for the Australian lower house. Here the constituency system is as above, but the voter puts a preference ordering against the candidates. If no candidate wins an outright majority of first preferences, the candidate with the fewest votes is eliminated, and his or her ballot papers are reallocated according to second preferences. This process continues until one candidate achieves a majority of the votes. A majority result can also be achieved by holding a second ballot in which only the top two candidates from the first round of voting go into the second (as in France).

The single transferable vote

The single transferable vote is used in Ireland, Malta and the Australian Senate. Here the constituencies return a number of members, usually between three and seven according to population density. Voters have as many votes as there are representatives to be elected, which they list in order of preference. To be elected a candidate has to achieve a certain 'quota' or proportion of the votes cast. Those who fail to achieve the quota on the first preferences may do so on second and later-order preferences, according to a given formula for the redistribution of these preferences.

The party list

The party list system is used in most countries of Western Europe and in Israel. The parties draw up regional or national lists of candidates in a ranking order, and the voter casts one vote for his or her favoured party. Candidates are then elected in proportion to the total votes cast for the respective parties. A party may be required to achieve a minimum proportion of the vote to win any representation.

The mixed member system

The mixed member, or additional member, system is used in Germany and Hungary, and is proposed for New Zealand. Under this system a proportion of representatives (at least 50 per cent) is elected in single-member constituencies, as in the first two systems above. The remaining representatives are elected under a party list system, either regional or national, in such a manner as to make the total result as nearly 'proportional' to the distribution of the party vote as possible. Electors have two votes, one for a candidate and one for a party. Again there may be a minimum threshold which parties have to reach in order to qualify for representation.

29 What are the advantages and disadvantages of these systems?

The precise merits of different electoral systems cannot adequately be assessed separately from the character and distribution of a country's population and the pattern of electoral support for its different parties. For example, if a country lacks established political parties altogether, then a 'proportional' electoral system makes no sense, since it is the distribution of the popular vote between the parties that constitutes the focus of proportionality. The following assessment should therefore be read as identifying the general tendencies of the different systems, rather than their inevitable effects.

Simplicity

The *plurality* system (first past the post) has the merit of simplicity. It is more likely than other systems to produce single-party majorities in parliament, and hence single-party government, since it exaggerates the electoral support for the largest party. It is also able to register small shifts in electoral opinion to bring about a change of government, though this effect will depend upon the number of 'marginal' constituencies. The disadvantage of the system is that it can produce extremely disproportionate outcomes, depending on how the national vote is distributed between the parties and between the different constituencies. Thus, for example, if every constituency mirrored exactly a national distribution of support between four parties in the ratio 40, 30, 20, 10, then one party could win all the seats in parliament, leaving 60 per cent of the voters totally unrepresented. Of course this never happens. But the system favours parties whose vote is concentrated in certain areas, rather than thinly spread, and puts a considerable premium on how constituency boundaries are drawn. It also encourages voters to vote tactically, not necessarily voting for their first choice, but with arbitrary results, since they cannot know with certainty how other voters will behave.

Majority support

The *alternative vote* has the advantage over the plurality system that it requires a candidate to win a majority of votes in a constituency in order to be elected, whereas the plurality system does not. Winning such a majority could be seen as a minimum requirement for legitimately representing a constituency. Its broad effect is also likely to be more proportional than the plurality system. However, it could still prevent third and fourth parties with a substantial but evenly spread support from being represented in parliament.

Voter choice

The *single transferable vote* enables smaller parties to achieve representation, though how proportionately will depend upon the size of the constituencies (the larger, the more porportionate). Supporters of a given party are also able to express preferences between its candidates. However, the large size of constituencies tends to break the link between representatives and their electorate that is found in single-member constituencies; and the mechanism for distributing lower-preference votes between the candidates is extraordinarily complicated.

Proportionality

The *party list* system can claim to give the most nearly equal weight to each vote, and thus to produce the distrubution of seats most proportionate to the votes cast for the respective parties. Its disadvantages are that there is no direct accountability of representatives to a given body of constituents, and that the electorate (and even party members) may have no influence over the ordering of a party's candidates on the list. Representatives may thus be beholden more to the central party organization than to the electorate. The list system does, however, give parties both the opportunity and the incentive to produce a 'balanced' slate of candidates, as between different party tendencies and between different social groups.

Differential representation

The *mixed member* system can produce more or less proportionate outcomes according to what proportion of representatives are elected in single-member constituencies. It could thus be designed to produce single-party government when there is a strong surge of support for one party, while requiring coalition government in the event of a more even distribution of the popular vote. Besides the disadvantages of the list system, however, it also requires two different kinds of representative, those with constituencies and those without. Supporters of the system argue that these disadvantages can be overcome by constructing the party lists from the best losers in the constituency contests, and by allocating these members to given constituencies for constituency responsibilities.

30 Is coalition government undemocratic?

Supporters of proportional representation argue that the plurality and alternative vote systems are undemocratic because they treat the votes of citizens very unequally, allowing much greater weight to some than to others. They thus infringe the basic democratic principle of political equality. In doing so they can allow governments to be elected which only have the support of a minority of the electorate, sometimes a quite small minority. On the other side critics of proportional representation contend that, because it is rare for any single party ever to win a majority of the popular vote, under such a system coalition government will always be required. And coalitions take the determination of governments out of the hands of the electors and give it to the party bosses, thus reducing the degree of popular control and accountability. They may also give a disproportionate amount of power to minority parties, especially if they occupy a 'hinge' position in the centre between larger parties of left and right. To this it may be objected in turn that all parties will have to account to their electorates for the coalition decisions they make, and that centre parties cannot simply ignore the relative shift in votes between parties of the left and right from one election to the next.

Particular circumstances

Once more, it is difficult to decide upon the balance of the argument in abstraction from a particular country and its circumstances. The recent history of the UK has exposed the inadequacies of the simple plurality system as clearly as the recent history of Italy has shown the deficiencies of a purely proportional one. It may well be that a system which combines the strengths of constituency representation with some counterbalancing element of proportionality is likely to prove most generally serviceable, though the precise relation between the two must depend upon the context of party development and the wider constitutional arrangements.

31 How can the fairness of the election process be guaranteed?

There are three main sources of threat to the fairness of the election process. The first is the advantage that being in government gives to the ruling party or parties. This can never be entirely eliminated, but it can be minimized by a number of measures. Most important is that the whole election process – from the drawing of electoral boundaries, through the registration of voters and the conduct of the campaign, to the election itself and the counting of votes – should be supervised by an independent electoral commission, whose membership should require the approval of all political parties. Among its duties should be to regulate the access of parties to the publicly owned media during the campaign, if there is not an independent broadcasting commission to do so. Also of importance is that the organization of parties should be legally separated from the organization of government, and that ministers be required to surrender all official duties and privileges for the duration of the election campaign, other than those necessary to the guarantee of law and order in its conduct.

Electoral malpractice

A second threat to the fairness of the election process stems from all kinds of malpractice by party members and their supporters, including bribery, intimidation, impersonation, double voting, and so on. These can only be avoided if adequate personnel, both police and election officials, are assigned to ensure the physical security of candidates and the integrity of the election process. Of particular importance is the calibre of election officials, whose appointment and training should be the responsibility of the national electoral commission. The presence of experienced international observers may be of particular assistance; indeed there is a good argument for making their presence a standard feature of national elections in all democratic countries, to act as both an external guarantor of fair conduct and a disseminator of best electoral practice.

Influence of wealth

A final main threat to the fairness of the election process arises from the advantage that the possession of personal wealth or access to wealthy backers can give to individual candidates or parties. The simplest way to offset this is to set strict limits to the amounts of money that can be spent by and on behalf of candidates and parties, both nationally and locally, and to provide them all with free access to the publicly owned media, according to guidelines approved by the electoral commission or its equivalent.

Opinion polls

Of lesser threats to electoral fairness, the operation of opinion polls is under discussion in a number of countries. Some already have legislation banning the publication of opinion polls during the last week of an election or over the election period as a whole. The assumption is that such polls can affect the outcome of the election itself, through either a 'bandwagon' or 'counter-bandwagon' effect, and that they encourage an unhealthy concentration on the anticipated result to the exclusion of the issues which should determine it. However, most experts are sceptical about the influence of opinion polls on voting, and are doubtful about the practicability of suppressing them when people increasingly have access to the international media.

32 Should political parties be publicly funded?

The main arguments in favour of the public financing of political parties are that they play a vital political role in a democratic system, which should be recognized by financial support; and that public funding would diminish the influence of powerful vested interests on the political process. Parties could be financed in proportion to the votes cast for them in each national election; and public finance could be denied to a party that campaigned to deprive any group of its civil and political rights or that was convicted of electoral malpractice.

Party autonomy

The chief argument against public funding is that political parties can only be an effective vehicle for popular opinion from below to the extent that they maintain their autonomy from the state; and voluntary funding is a necessary condition for such autonomy. If parties cannot maintain sufficient support for their activities from voluntary contributions, then they do not deserve to be considered seriously for public office. At the same time, the undue influence of special interests can be curtailed if all donations to a party above a certain amount must be publicly declared, and if all institutional supporters are required to obtain the explicit agreement of their members, shareholders, etc. for any donations they make.

Limited public support

Most established democracies expect their parties to be financed from voluntary sources. However, this need not exclude limited public finance for carefully defined activities, such as the training of party cadres or free access to the publicly owned media at election time. Such financial support may be particularly necessary in a period of transition to democracy, when parties may have to be started from scratch and there is little recent experience of electoral competition.

33 Should elected representatives be allowed to change their party allegiance between elections?

No. By standing for election under given party labels, candidates are in effect committing themselves to the support of those parties for the term of office. If that were not so, the use of the vote to choose between different programmes and political tendencies would be rendered meaningless. In an electoral system organized on a constituency basis, anyone seeking to change party allegiance should be required to resign and fight a by-election. In a 'list' system he or she would simply have to resign and be replaced by the next candidate on the list of the same party.

34 Do voters have any power between elections?

It is mistaken to imagine that because the only political act voters may undertake is to cast their votes once every four years or so they are powerless in between. The *prospect* of having to face the electorate in the future constitutes an important discipline on governing parties, and compels them to consult public opinion on a continuous basis. In other words, elections cast long shadows in front of them. This is particularly evident in a constituency-based electoral system, where defeat for a governing party in a by-election may lead to dramatic changes of policy and even of leadership. In addition, there exist a variety of channels for voters to exert influence over the government on specific issues between elections, such as membership of pressure groups and voluntary associations, contributing to public campaigns, contacting representatives and members of the government, taking part in demonstrations, and so on. And the media constitute a decisive instrument for the continuous organization and expression of public opinion.

35 When should referenda be held in a democracy?

Most democracies require referenda to be held, sometimes by qualified majority, in the event of a proposed change to the constitution or of legislation that has substantial constitutional implications. The reason is that a constitution belongs to the people as a whole, not to members of parliament or the government of the day; and it should therefore be subject to direct popular approval.

Referenda on other legislation

Having referenda on other, substantive issues of policy or legislation is more debatable. Those in favour of the use of referenda argue that they constitute an important democratic device, which allows the population a direct say on important issues that may otherwise be simply ignored or lost in the generality of a party's election manifesto. Against this, it can be contended that, since so many issues of political decision are interconnected (e.g. taxation and public spending), it is quite arbitrary to take one issue out of context and require its resolution by a group of people different from those who have the responsibility for all the other decisions. It is in effect a sign of no confidence in the representative process, which is more likely to reduce than to enhance the accountability of elected representatives.

No right answer

This is one of those issues where there is no right or wrong answer, and democracies will adopt different practices according to their own political traditions.

3 | Open and Accountable Government

36 Why is open government important to democracy?

Open government is essential to democracy because public officials cannot be held accountable, nor citizens make an informed electoral choice, unless there is accurate information available about the activity of the government and the consequences of its policies. Access to such information should be seen as a right of citizens and of the media on their behalf, rather than as a favour of governments, since it is the electorate which pays the bills to keep the government going; it should therefore know what it is getting for its money and what is being done in its name. Although providing such access is often criticized as itself a drain on public resources, it has its own contribution to make to government efficiency, in helping to expose waste, to inhibit corruption and to identify policy errors before they become chronic. It is also an important element in the protection of civil liberties that individuals should have access to personal files held on them by the government and its agencies.

Aspects of open government

What exactly does open government involve? Open government can be seen as having four main strands. First is the provision by the government itself of factual information about its policies: the evidence on which they are based, their consequences in practice, their cost, the rules governing their operation, and so on. Second is the access of individuals and the press to government documents, both directly and indirectly through parliament; this will include the accessibility of personal files to the individuals concerned. Third is the openness of meetings to the public and the press; this can typically range from parliament and its committees to the proceedings of publicly funded agencies and the meetings of local government. Fourth is the systematic consultation by the government of relevant interests in the formulation and implementation of policy, and the publication of the information and advice so received.

Legitimate exceptions

Are there any exceptions to the principle of open government? The categories of information that are usually justified in a democracy as legitimately confidential include: the deliberations of cabinet; political advice given to ministers by civil servants; information whose publication would damage national defence, the security of the democratic system or the physical safety of individuals; trade secrets of private firms; personal files, except to the individuals concerned.

37 How can open government be secured?

In the pre-twentieth-century era of limited government it was thought sufficient for ensuring open government that

63

the freedom of the press was guaranteed. Nowadays, with much more complex and far-reaching state activity, even the most stringent guarantees of press freedom, including provision for protecting the confidentiality of journalists' sources, are insufficient on their own. The characteristic tendency of governments and their bureaucracies is to cloak their activities in secrecy, so as to protect error or misdemeanour, to avoid embarrassment, or simply to preserve their conviction that they know best. This tendency can nowadays only be effectively counteracted by legislation requiring open government, or 'freedom of information'.

Freedom of information

Model legislation for freedom of information, setting standards of 'best practice', is provided by the USA and Sweden. This covers all the main areas mentioned earlier (see question 36): the duty of government disclosure; the right of public access to documents; the openness of meetings of public agencies; also the protection of 'whistle-blowers', who leak evidence of malpractice or illegality within the government service. Such legislation should be seen as additional and complementary to measures guaranteeing the right of parliament or the legislature to scrutinize the executive. An important feature of such legislation is that the interpretation of the exceptions to disclosure (e.g. those necessary to national security, to protect privacy, etc.) is vested with the courts rather than with the government itself.

Public relations expenditure

Two further issues deserve mention. First, modern governments are characterized by the enormous budgets devoted to 'public relations'. This embraces not only factual information about government policy, but also its timing and presentation so as to maximize favourable impact, the practice of selective

leaking, and all the other devices in the public relations armoury used to massage public opinion. These practices make the guarantee of independent access to, and testing of, government information especially crucial. Of particular importance here is the existence of a public statistical service, independent of the government, on which the government, parliament and the public can draw equally.

Public consultation

Finally, open government as a concept is much broader than simple freedom of information. It includes the accessibility of ministers to debate and justify their policies in public, and the degree to which the government is required to consult the public in its formulation and implementation of policy. This latter involves legislation covering such issues as: requisite timescales and procedures for consultation; the publication of evidence from interested parties; the assessment of environmental impact; and so forth. 'Openness' thus comprises the readiness to listen as well as to make available access to accurate information.

38   What is meant by accountable government?

The concept of accountable government has three main dimensions.

Legal accountability

First is *legal accountability*: the accountability of all public officials, elected and non-elected, to the courts for the legality of their actions. Here lies the basic meaning of the 'rule of law', that those who make and execute law and policy must

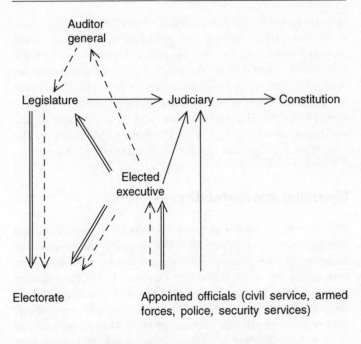

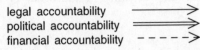

Figure 2   Accountability routes

themselves act under and within the law and the constitution, on the basis of powers which are legally defined and circumscribed.

Political accountability

The second aspect is *political accountability*: the accountability of the government or executive to parliament and public for the justifiability of its policies, their prioritization and their manner of execution. Where the first, legal, type of account- ability has a relatively simple structure, as between public

67

officials and the courts, political accountability is more complex. Non-elected agencies of government at national level
(the civil service, armed forces, police, security services) are
typically accountable to the elected head of the executive
through ministers appointed by him or her. The chief executive and ministers are accountable in turn both to the public
directly via the electoral process, and to parliament or the
legislature acting as agents of the public. Members of the
legislature are then accountable to their own electorate.

Financial accountability

Third is the narrower concept of *financial accountability*: the
accountability of a government for spending the proceeds of
taxation only on those purposes approved by the legislature,
and in the most cost-effective manner. Here the route of
accountability follows closely that of political accountability,
with the important addition of an auditor general's office,
which is accountable to parliament but acts independently of
it in its professional scrutiny of the detail of government
expenditure.

Accountability and popular control

These different accountability routes are traced in diagram-
matic form in figure 2. Whereas each of them contributes to
the democratic principle of popular control over government,
it will be seen that both financial and legal accountability are
best secured through professional bodies that operate with a
certain degree of immunity from direct public or political
influence, and that are accountable to their own professional
codes of practice. Ultimately, however, it is political accountability that is supreme, since the legislation which the courts
enforce and the expenditure which the auditor general scruti-
nizes are themselves dependent upon the authorization of a
popularly elected parliament, acting under the constitution.

39 Why is the separation of powers important?

In democracies government is divided into three branches: the executive (sometimes also called 'the government' *simpliciter*), which is responsible for the formulation and execution of policy; the legislature (also called parliament, representative or national assembly), which is responsible for the approval of legislation and taxation and the scrutiny of the executive; the judiciary (or the courts), which is responsible for securing the observance of the law, by determining whether it has been infringed and sentencing those found guilty of its infringement. This separation of the three branches has proved essential to secure the different forms of accountability mentioned above (see question 38). Thus, if the courts are not independent of both legislature and executive, they cannot act without fear or favour to ensure that public officials operate within the law. Similarly, if parliament does not have independent powers to approve legislation and taxation and to scrutinize the executive, the political and financial accountability of the government to the electorate will be seriously impaired.

Different systems

Although the separation of powers between executive and legislature is a common feature of democratic government, it is treated differently in the various political systems. In a presidential system, where the chief executive is elected separately from the legislature and has no place in it, the separation between the two is most sharply defined. In a prime-ministerial system, on the other hand, in which the chief executive is chosen as the party leader who can command a parliamentary majority, he or she has a foot in both camps as it were: acting both as head of the executive branch and as leader of the majority in parliament.

Presidentialism

Each system has its advantages and disadvantages. The advantage of the presidential system lies typically in the much greater independence of the legislature in its ability to control the executive, although this will also vary according to the degree of organization of political parties and the balance of party control between the two branches. The corresponding disadvantage lies in what has come to be called 'gridlocked' government: the inability of the executive to secure the necessary legislation and taxation to carry out the policies on which it was directly elected. In extreme circumstances this separation may result in a struggle for power between the two branches, in which the president may be tempted to use his or her directly elected authority, together with the control of the military, in a plebiscitary coup against the legislature.

Parliament and executive

The advantage of the prime-ministerial system lies in its greater ability to coordinate executive policy with the necessary legislation and taxation, and in the much greater unlikelihood of an executive coup against parliament (a feature that may be particularly relevant to a democratic system only recently established). The corresponding disadvantage lies in the ability of the executive to control the parliamentary agenda, and to limit its scrutinizing function, since members of the parliamentary majority usually have a much greater interest in maintaining the credibility of the government (on which their own seats and future promotion prospects depend) than in exposing its defects to public view.

40 What is the rule of law and how can it be guaranteed?

The rule of law embodies the simple principle that all state officials, whether elected or non-elected, should act within the law and the constitution, on the basis of powers that are legally defined and circumscribed (see legal accountability, question 38). The principle can be traced back to the Aristotelian idea that the best government involves the 'rule of laws, not of men'. In its modern form the principle evolved from the struggle to limit the arbitrary discretion of the monarch and his or her officials, by requiring legal authorization for all executive action.

Democracy and rule of law

The rule of law can be readily seen to be a cornerstone of both individual freedom and democracy. Without it there can be no protection of individual rights from the executive. And, in so far as the *source* of law is a democratic constitution and an elected legislature, it must be a requirement of democracy that the executive observe it. Attempts to bypass procedural or legal regularity 'in the national interest' or under the pressure of instant popular demand must therefore be judged undemocratic.

Independence of the judiciary

The rule of law is only effective, however, to the extent that there is an independent judiciary to uphold it. Article 1 of the UN Basic Principles on the Judiciary states that 'the independence of the judiciary shall be guaranteed by the state and enshrined in the constitution or the laws of the country'. This independence is both a collective independence of the institution of the judiciary from interference by the executive,

71

and also the personal independence of individual judges to perform their offices without fear or favour. Both kinds of independence require more than formal constitutional guarantees; they depend also on the methods by which judges are appointed and on the security of their tenure of office. Appointments should not be in the hands of the government or executive, but should be the responsibility of a judicial committee of parliament or of an independent judicial services committee established under the constitution. Similarly, judges should not be dismissable by the government of the day but have security of tenure that is terminable only by a special procedure of the appointing body, and for limited causes such as corruption or other gross misdemeanour or dereliction of duty. Similar considerations apply to other branches of the legal profession, whose independence from government is necessary to secure the principle of the rule of law.

41 What contribution does parliament or the legislature make to government accountability?

Parliament plays the central role in ensuring the political and financial accountability of the executive. It does this, in the first place, through its powers to approve legislation and taxation and through the procedures which ensure that all measures before it are thoroughly tested and debated before becoming law. Second are the powers of parliament to scrutinize the work of the executive: through questioning ministers, inspecting documents and cross-examining relevant state personnel. These functions are carried out both by parliament sitting as a whole and through an organized structure of committees.

Parliamentary effectiveness

The effectiveness with which parliament carries out its role
of ensuring the government's accountability depends partly
upon the independent-mindedness of individual members.
Traditionally, it was thought sufficient to guarantee their
independence if they were given immunity from prosecution
for anything they said in parliament, so that they could speak
their minds fearlessly. Given the complexity of government
business today, however, representatives can only be effectively critical if they have sufficient research and office facilities
and ready access to external expertise. It is also important
that they are not so tied to party positions that their critical
faculties become blunted. Where members are dependent
upon a party hierarchy either for their initial election or for
their appointment to specialist committees, they are much
less likely to step out of line.

Role of the opposition

However, we should not ignore the important place the organized party system has in the scrutiny of government. It is the
task of an official opposition not only to act as an alternative
'government in waiting', but also to coordinate the scrutiny of
government through subjecting its work to sustained criticism. Many people find this the least attractive feature of a
parliament's work, since it often conveys the impression of
'opposition for opposition's sake', regardless of the merits of
any particular government measure. This impression is indeed
well founded, particularly in the adversarial British system
and those parliaments derived from it. Yet, just as modern
government is highly organized, so must be the process of
scrutinizing it; and this responsibility particularly falls on those
parties that do not support the government in power, who
should be able to criticize the government fearlessly without
their patriotism being brought into question.

42 Can anyone become a member of parliament?

We elect representatives not for any special expertise they may possess but because we trust them to do a conscientious job in defending constituents' interests, in scrutinizing the work and the proposals of the government and in promoting the programme on which they have been elected. Any reasonably intelligent, conscientious, organized and articulate person is capable of doing this, whatever walk of life he or she comes from. Once elected, representatives will have access to the time and the resources necessary to do the job effectively. Over time they will also gain experience; but it is a necessary condition of electoral accountability that the job is not one that can be guaranteed for life.

Individual competition

Although many people, therefore, could do the job of a representative, very few actually do. The route to doing so is typically lengthy and arduous. Almost invariably they will need to belong to an established political party and to have worked for it for a number of years, often with experience of elected office at local or sub-national level. They will then need to convince a party selection board or committee of their suitability, in competition with others, and will probably have to stand unsuccessfully in one or two elections before they achieve winnable seats or positions on the party list. Even then, it might turn out to be a bad year for the party! So it requires a lot of determination as well as luck. Only those with a very strong interest in public affairs and a readiness to work unsocial hours will last the course.

43 Should elected representatives be allowed to hold other paid employment?

The arguments typically advanced in favour are that parliament is not a full-time job throughout the year; that a parliamentary income on its own is insufficient to attract the most talented people into politics; that outside employment helps keep members in touch with the 'real world'. None of these arguments is at all convincing. Although parliament may not sit throughout the year, its work is continuous and demanding, and can only be done properly on a full-time basis. Voters should expect this to be so, and should be prepared to pay for a salary appropriate to the responsibility and for the necessary facilities to be provided. The most effective way in which elected members can stay in touch with the real world is to meet their constituents from every section of society on a regular basis and listen to what they have to say.

Sectional interests

Should representatives be paid fees or 'retainers' by outside bodies to represent their interests in parliament? Although this practice is widespread in many parliaments, it is also undesirable. It is difficult to see how members can conscientiously represent the interests of their electorate if at the same time they are being paid by special groups, often at national level, to work on their behalf. Requiring a public register of such payments is less preferable than prohibiting them altogether.

Termination of office

A characteristic feature of a representative's position is that it may be terminated abruptly by the electorate, not necessarily for any failing on the individual's part, but because the party's leader and programme are no longer acceptable. Actually this is not all that different from employees in private industry being made suddenly redundant because of market changes that are none of their fault. Both types of worker should have access to decent severance pay, according to the years worked, to enable them to find alternative employment; and they should enjoy transferable pension rights.

44 How can political corruption be eradicated?

Political corruption – the abuse of public office for private gain – can occur at any level of government and in any political system. Although in some democracies it may be condoned as the expected 'perks of office', and taken for granted in the competition for government contracts or the award of trading licences, it destroys the trust between representatives and their constituents and undermines confidence in the democratic process, to the point where people may not think democracy worth defending. For this reason it has to be treated seriously, and efforts made to minimize it, even if it can never be completely eradicated.

Remedial measures

Political corruption tends to flourish in the following conditions: where the pay for public office is comparatively low or inadequate, or where, alternatively, it constitutes the only societal avenue to a decent income; where economic oppor-

tunities in the private sector are particularly dependent upon discretionary government decisions; and where the chances of being exposed and punished are low. The above conditions suggest their corresponding antidotes: to pay public officials decently, though not excessively in comparison with other jobs; to subject all government decisions affecting private economic agents to clearly defined rules and procedures; and to combine open government with fearless judicial investigation of suspected illegality. The best inoculation against corruption is the development over time of a culture and tradition of disinterested public service that is not penetrated too far by the market philosophy of self-interest maximization. None of these measures, least of all the last, is easy where the problem has become chronic and deep-seated.

45 What role does the civil service play in a democracy?

The full-time non-elected officials of the civil service constitute the permanent administration on which a government relies for getting its day-to-day business conducted. They provide both the expert advice necessary to the formulation of policy and legislation, and the administrative structure necessary to carrying it out effectively. They are expected to perform these roles conscientiously and impartially, whatever party or parties are in government and whether they agree personally with the tendency of government policy or not. Although a professional civil service is characteristic of every contemporary system of government, a number of issues arise which are particular to the organization of a civil service in a democracy, such as: how the senior civil servants are appointed; to whom civil servants should be accountable; and the pattern of their recruitment.

Political appointments

The first of these issues arises out of a concern expressed within many political parties that, precisely because some higher civil servants are not committed to the policies of the party in power, they may act to obstruct it, or use their monopoly of expertise to provide 'loaded' advice to ministers, who are typically much less expert than their advisers. These concerns are often overstated. It is the responsibility of civil servants to test every policy proposal against objections and practical difficulties, as well as to find ways of carrying it out; and this can often be interpreted as obstructionism. However, it is also true that the civil service constitutes a powerful non-elected influence on policy, and that this influence is capable of being used undemocratically. Established democracies generally use one of two methods to minimize this possibility. One is to make the top administrative post or posts in each ministry subject to political appointment, in principle changing with every change in the elected government. The other is the establishment of a political office in each ministry, staffed by specialists who are also party supporters, who can provide alternative advice and information to the minister, and who have the expertise to provide an independent check on the advice offered by the permanent civil service. Neither method is entirely problem-free, but the advantages probably outweigh the disadvantages.

Civil service accountability

A second issue concerns the accountability of civil servants. All civil service bureaucracies are organized hierarchically, with accountability upwards to a superior, and ultimately to the relevant minister, and through the minister to parliament. But do not civil servants in a democracy also have a *direct* responsibility to the law, to parliament and to the public, which may on occasion transcend their accountability to superiors? What if the instructions they receive involve a breach of the law, or the deception of parliament, or an infringement of the rights of clients of the services they are providing? Such examples demonstrate the possibility of a clear conflict between bureaucratic and democratic principles of accountability. In practice many civil servants resolve such conflicts by means of the 'unofficial leak'. Here is one reason for the importance of a law to protect 'whistle-blowers' (see question 37).

Recruitment of public servants

A final issue about the civil service in a democracy is its pattern of recruitment. Quality of entrants is typically secured by competitive selection from those with higher education or relevant professional training and expertise, independently of any party allegiance. However, while this ensures a certain intellectual exclusivity to recruitment, it is important that it should not also be socially exclusive. The public service in a democracy should both be and be seen to be fairly represent-ative of the main groups within society. And the principle of political equality requires that access to public appointment be equally open to all, regardless of which social group they belong to. This means that anti-discrimination and equal-opportunities policies should be effective within the education system as well as in recruitment to the civil service itself.

46 What contribution can individual citizens make to accountable government?

In a democratic system individual citizens have important avenues of redress against government officials in the event of damage to their interests through unlawful decisions or maladministration (neglect, delay, arbitrariness, etc.). For decisions taken beyond a government's legally defined powers there is redress through the courts. In cases of maladministration there is the possibility of rectification through appeal to the constituent's elected representative, or through the office of an ombudsman, who has specific responsibility for assessing the validity of individual grievances against executive decisions. Most recently developed has been the institution of the 'citizen's charter', whereby people are compensated for specific failures of a government service to meet designated standards. All these can be seen as examples of consumer accountability, initiated by the individual, in contrast to the other more corporate forms of accountability already discussed (see question 38). They serve as an important reminder that the chief customer for government services is the public at large, and that the ultimate focus for the process of legal, political and financial accountability of a government is the citizens themselves.

47 How can the armed forces be kept subject to civilian control?

In long-established democracies, with a well-understood and carefully protected separation between political and military decisions, this hardly seems a major problem, except in occasional borderline disputes over weapons procurement, manning levels or conditions of service in the armed forces. In a recently established democracy, on the other hand, which may have experienced a history of *coups d'état*, of military rule, or of military veto over the personnel or policy of the government, the problem may come to seem insuperable. After all, the military everywhere have the physical and organizational *capacity* to depose elected politicians, to take over the government and to subject the population at large to their rule. The question, therefore, is one of their *willingness* to do so, and how this can be discouraged.

Military coups

Maintaining military subordination to elected politicians is rarely a simple question of training them in a non-political role, or keeping them satisfied with pay and status and advanced technical weaponry. Internal dissatisfaction within the armed forces may be a contributory factor in *coups d'état*, but it is rarely the decisive one. They will usually take over civilian government only when there is a deep and sustained crisis in the democratic order that the politicians have proved incapable of resolving: civil war, chronic inflation, breakdown of public order, flagrant and persistent political corruption. Military coups may also take place to pre-empt parties with radical programmes that threaten the established order of things from winning at the polls or from exercising office. In either case a failure in the consolidation of workable democratic institutions is the root cause, not some inherent character of the military as such.

Military rule

Military rule can at best, however, provide only a short-term palliative to society's problems, not a long-term solution. A decade or two ago it was fashionable to exalt the military as the chief agency of economic modernization and nation building, in contrast to the corruption and divisiveness of democratic politics. Yet the armed forces are simply incapable of providing a source of legitimate authority for government. And their record in power is dismal. Closed and secretive government may merely conceal corruption, rather than reduce it, and it has proved no basis for sound economic management; and the military in power have a record of human rights abuses which no system of open government could tolerate.

Democratic consolidation

There is no serious alternative to the long road of consolidating democratic institutions, constitutional government and the rule of law, with international support if need be, or to seeking to resolve major societal conflicts through the political means of negotiation and compromise. At the same time there need to be developed more effective methods, at both national and international levels, for identifying and punishing serious human rights abuses, especially those perpetrated by state personnel, and for instituting sanctions against the regimes that permit them.

48 Is there any place for a secret service in a democracy?

Democracy is in principle antithetical to secrecy anywhere in government. However, democratic states have always found it necessary to mount covert operations to protect society against external threat, internal organized crime and conspiracy to subvert the democratic process itself. The problem with such operations is that the methods employed – surveillance, bugging, telephone-tapping, dirty tricks of all kinds – constitute an infringement of individuals' civil rights, and that, precisely because they are so secretive, they can readily cross the boundary of publicly justifiable targets to include political organizations and activities that are perfectly legal, but which happen to be troublesome to a particular government and its policies.

Political accountability

Everything therefore hangs on the issue of political control. It is not sufficient for security operations to be covered in the general accountability of the relevant minister or ministers to parliament. There needs to be a special committee of parliament, meeting as necessary in secret, to supervise such activities and ensure that publicly justifiable guidelines are being adhered to. And the ombudsman should have the power to investigate complaints from people who have grounds for believing that their civil rights are being infringed in the surveillance of perfectly legitimate activities.

85

49 Why is local government important to democracy?

Having a system of elected local government is important to the vitality of a democratic system for a number of reasons. It greatly expands the opportunities for taking part in public decision-making, and the number of those involved in it. Because it is locally based, it is much more responsive to the particularity of local needs and circumstances than national government can be. It allows for small-scale experiments in policy, which if successful can be copied elsewhere, at national level or otherwise. It provides a stepping stone for politicians to national office and a political base for parties that have been defeated nationally. Finally, by limiting the concentration of power in the hands of central government, it adds a spatial dimension to the constitutional separation of powers. Each of these features on its own is significant; taken together, they add up to an unanswerable case for elected local government.

Centralizing tendencies

However, in contemporary states there are powerful forces at work which encourage the centralization of political decision-making. There is the pressure from treasury departments seeking to control the overall level of public expenditure as an essential instrument of national economic management. There is the reluctance of national politicians to allow political opponents at local level to obstruct or dilute central policy initiatives. Then there are the expectations of the public at large, who in an increasingly mobile society become intolerant of significant variations in the standards of services from one locality to the next. Equality of citizenship means equality in the standards of service; if this can only be achieved by a substantial redistribution of resources between different areas, as well as by national regulation, then this considerably restricts the autonomy of local government, and with it the scope of local electoral choice.

Competing imperatives

There is no easy solution to these competing imperatives, or one that is universally applicable. However, since the most powerful pressures today come from the direction of centralization, it is the interests of local government and locality that most stand in need of protection. At a minimum this might require: a clear separation of functions between centre and locality that is intelligible to the electorate; sufficient powers and resources to carry out these functions according to local needs and circumstances, albeit within the framework of national regulations; adequate mechanisms of accountability to the local electorate; that the central government should not interfere in the discretion of local authorities, and that if necessary this should be enforced through a constitutional court. At the end of the day, however, effective relations between centre and locality depend upon cooperation and a mutual recognition of each other's spheres, rather than narrow legalism.

50 When is federalism desirable?

Federalism involves the division of a national territory into separate states, each with its own elected parliament and executive and the right to legislate and raise taxes according to a constitutionally guaranteed division of powers between it and the government at national level. Historically, federal states have come into being in a number of ways: through the amalgamation of previously sovereign states; through the granting of autonomy to regions or nations within a previously unitary state; through the settlement of an original founding convention.

Regional differences

Federalism is usually desirable in territorially large states that contain wide variations in culture and geography between their constituent regions. It also offers a potential solution anywhere to demands for autonomy from culturally or ethnically distinct minorities living within the same geographical area, as an alternative to outright independence. Living 'semi-detached' may be preferable both to complete detachment and to continuous squabbling under the same roof. Many of the arguments advanced in favour of elected local government (see question 49) can be seen to apply with equal force to federal systems.

4 | Individual Rights and Their Defence

51 What are human rights?

Human rights and fundamental freedoms are individual entitlements derived from human needs and capacities. The recognition of human rights and the creation of means for their defence in international law constitute perhaps the most important moral advance of this century. The international community has adopted many international agreements or conventions on human rights. These instruments seek to establish agreed definitions about the scope of human rights and freedoms and at the same time commit governments to take the necessary steps to ensure that such rights are protected in law and practice in their respective countries.

The Universal Declaration

The main source of human rights ideas in the modern world stems from the *Universal Declaration of Human Rights*, adopted by the United Nations General Assembly on 10 December 1948. In 1966 the United Nations adopted two international instruments based on the rights proclaimed in the Universal Declaration. These are the International Covenant on Economic Social and Cultural Rights and the International Covenant on Civil and Political Rights. Two-thirds of the world's states have now ratified these instruments. The UN also adopted an Optional Protocol to the International Civil and Political Covenant, which provides individuals with a right of petition to the monitoring body for this Covenant, the Human Rights Committee, if their rights were violated by their governments. But this right is available only if the state in question, having ratified that Covenant, has also accepted this Protocol. Not so many states have done so.

Regional conventions

These instruments, the *Universal Declaration of Human Rights*, the two Covenants and the Optional Protocol are together known as the International Bill of Human Rights. There are many other universal national treaties on human rights as well as regional conventions, such as the American Convention on Human Rights, the African Charter on Human and People's Rights and the European Convention on Human Rights, which cannot be discussed here. Suggestions for further reading on human rights can be found at the end of the book.

52 How are rights classified?

Rights can be classified in many ways, but the most accepted is into civil, political, social, economic and cultural rights. This is the classification adopted in the International Bill of Human Rights. Examples of civil and political rights are: the right to life, freedom from torture, freedom from forced labour, freedom from arbitrary arrest, the right to fair trial, freedom of thought, conscience, religion or belief, the right to private life, the freedoms of speech and association and the right to take part in public affairs. Civil and political rights are typically rights that require a state to refrain from action or interference with individuals or groups. However, they can also impose obligations of action on a state, for example to fund a legal aid system to ensure that the poor or those of limited means can defend their rights in court, for example when they face serious criminal charges. Another example might be public expenditure to ensure that a national minority has access to the media.

Economic, social and cultural rights

Examples of economic, social and cultural rights are the rights to food and to health, to an adequate standard of living, to equal pay for equal work, to social security, to work, to strike, to housing, to education and to participate in cultural life. Economic and social rights are typically rights that require a state to act or to provide, where individuals cannot provide for themselves, for example because they are unemployed or because they are disabled.

Freedom from discrimination

An important principle attached to all rights is that in exercising rights people should not be discriminated against on grounds such as sex, race, religion or belief.

53 Are some rights more important than others?

The best answer is that all internationally recognized human rights are interrelated and reinforce each other. In some societies, depending on their stage of development, certain rights may be taken for granted by most citizens, for example, in richer countries, the right to a reasonable standard of living and the rights to food, clothing, shelter and education. In poorer countries these rights will be uppermost in the concerns of the people. But in all democratic societies such economic and social rights are fundamental and should be guaranteed, just as basic civil and political rights, the right to be governed under the rule of law, to have protection from arbitrary arrest and detention and to enjoy freedom of expression and association are fundamental and should be guaranteed. In international law it is the duty of the state to promote respect for all human rights of all citizens without distinction.

54 Are human rights universal?

Yes, the international standards address common human needs and capacities of the individual everywhere in the world. The world is of course made up of different regions and cultures. It is also divided between poorer and richer countries. It has been argued that the international human rights standards, because they begin with the individual, are alien to cultures that do not see the individual as separate from the community and that emphasize the duty of the individual to the community first. Whether contemporary ideas of individual human rights are causing societies to reinterpret the relationship between communities and their members is a subject which is much debated, both in the North as well as in the South of the world. They probably are, but there is no evidence that the recognition or the protection of the individual's human rights damages human solidarity and community. To the contrary, the norms of universal human rights seek to protect human groups and peoples and recognize the need for individuals to join with others in the use of their own languages and to belong to and participate in their own cultures, religions and ways of life. International human rights law first recognizes a basic level of common entitlements to human rights for all human beings, but beyond that accepts and endorses the entitlement of all cultures to flourish, including those of indigenous peoples.

Rights and duties

The *Universal Declaration of Human Rights* also speaks of the individual's duties to his or her community. It asserts that it is only in community with others that an individual's free and full development of personality is possible. The notion of human rights nevertheless begins with the belief in the unique worth of every individual human person. (See also question 2.)

Non-selective standards

Some of the force behind the criticism of international human rights standards as universal aspirations comes less from a supposed clash between the world's cultures over whether priority should be given to an individual's rights or duties than from a supposed conflict over whether priority should be assigned to the individual or the community. It is clear that different balances can exist in different cultures with respect to these facets of human rights without negating their essential universality. Rather such criticism is fuelled by the undoubted evidence that governments worldwide are not even-handed in their treatment of human rights abuses. It is still commonplace for condemnation to be selective, depending on the power relations between states. In other words, too often states condemn the records of their opponents and overlook the records of their allies. If universal support for human rights and democracy is to be achieved, an international order based on respect for human rights must be based on a system of international accountability for upholding common global standards that is founded on principles of non-selectivity and objectivity in the exercise of judging the records of states.

Vienna Conference

These important understandings about human rights and about the duties of the international community were more recently confirmed at the World Conference on Human Rights held in Vienna in June 1993.

> All human rights are universal, indivisible and interdependent and inter-related. The international community must treat human rights globally in a fair and equal manner on the same footing and with the same emphasis. While the significance of national and regional particularities and various historical cultural and religious backgrounds must be borne in mind, it is the duty of states regardless of their political economic and cultural systems to promote and to protect all human rights and fundamental freedoms. (Concluding Document, para. 3.)

55 Is expression of international concern about a country's human rights record legitimate?

The principle of non-interference in the internal affairs of states by other states is one of the cardinal principles of the modern international order as laid down in the Charter of the United Nations. However, the growth of the international human rights movement and the steady extension of international human rights standards have brought about this currently accepted principle: that the way any state treats its citizens is in the public domain, and that external criticism from other governments or NGOs does not constitute interference in the internal affairs of that country. The World Conference on Human Rights confirmed that 'the promotion and protection of all human rights is a legitimate concern of the international community' (Concluding Document, para. 2.2).

56 What is the relation between human rights and democracy?

The World Conference on Human Rights spoke of the relation between human rights and democracy (along with that of development) as being 'inter-dependent and mutually reinforcing'. Another way of expressing this point is that it is now recognized by the international community that the protection of human rights and the rule of law, not only in developed but also in developing states, is best achieved through a commitment to democratic principles. It is also recognized that the exercise of human rights and freedoms is necessary for democracy to function properly at all. It used to be claimed that individual human rights could be defended and enjoyed in undemocratic systems, especially where the priority had to be given to economic development. But the evidence is overwhelming that such systems sooner rather than later become less benign, more repressive, corrupt and unstable.

Democratic government as a human right

The belief in the intimate relation between democracy and human rights is not new. The *Universal Declaration of Human Rights* included an endorsement of democratic government. It states as one of its ideals that 'the will of the people shall be the basis of the authority of government' (Article 21). The International Covenant on Civil and Political Rights requires states to guarantee for every citizen the right and opportunity to 'take part in the conduct of public affairs, directly or indirectly through chosen representatives, to vote and to be elected at genuine periodic elections [and] to have access on general terms of equality to public office' (Article 25).

Right to development

The unambiguous acknowledgment of the interdependent relation between the idea of universal human rights and that of democratic government is among the most important advances in international relations since the end of the Cold War. Equally, the general acceptance by the developing world of respect for human rights and democratic government as the basis for the achievement of the right to development has been a further positive advance in this period.

57 What is the relation between civil and political rights and democracy?

The guarantee of civil and political rights for the individual citizen plays a dual role in democracy. First, these rights are essential to secure the twin democratic principles of popular control and political equality in the system of collective decision-making. Secondly, such rights and freedoms act as a constraint on collective action by defining spheres of individual freedom and choice that are outside the reach of majority decision. This dual role is best illustrated by examining briefly some of the civil and political rights most intimately linked with the democratic system.

Liberty and security of the person

Without protection from arbitrary arrest, detention, banishment or expulsion, the individual cannot with security participate in political debate or action. This common-sense point is illustrated by the rule that members of the legislature are normally immune from arrest while engaged in parliamentary duties. But the need for respect for the right to liberty extends to all in a democracy. A democratic society defends the liberty and physical integrity of the unpopular individual, for example, even against the wishes of a majority.

'Due process'

Similar arguments can be made for the need to protect the citizen from unfair accusation, ill-treatment and torture and a biased trial. To prosecute political enemies is commonplace in societies that reject democracy. A democratic society requires an independent judiciary and an administration of criminal justice that is based on the rule of law and devoid of political and ideological influence and manipulation.

Freedom of thought and conscience

A democratic society presupposes that each individual is free to think as he or she wishes and to hold his or her own ideas, opinions and general philosophy of life. Equally a democratic society offers freedom for the individual to adhere along with others to a religion or belief and to practise and manifest beliefs subject only to the rights of others. Freedom of thought must always be protected as an individual right against what may be the prevailing and even the overwhelming majority's beliefs, whether it be of a religious or secular nature. In particular, minorities of different religions or beliefs are entitled to the same guarantees of freedom as the majority community.

Freedom of expression and of the media

The essence of democracy as we have defined it has been that each citizen has a voice that is equally entitled to be heard with all others. Freedom of speech is therefore an essential human right if each citizen is to have the opportunity to be heard. The international standards on freedom of speech concern not only the right to speak out but the right 'to seek and to receive information and ideas of all kinds, through any media regardless of frontiers'. In a modern society that means the mass media should be independent within clear rules established to protect individuals' reputations and privacy, and should be free to inform the citizen, criticize the government and to stimulate all manner of debate on policy choices (see question 6).

Freedom of information

The openness of government in a democracy is enhanced by the principle of freedom of information, that is that

government information and documentation are freely accessible to the public and, subject to narrow exceptions, are not classified as confidential or secret. (See question 37.)

Freedom of assembly and association

The modern representative democracy could not function without guarantees that people are free to come together to discuss public affairs, to form trade unions and other associations, to press their interests with the government and to form and participate in political parties. These freedoms include the right to congregate, to demonstrate and to petition for the redress of grievances.

58 How do social and economic rights relate to democracy?

In the democratic pyramid (see question 15), the fundamental rights which secure employment, housing, food, an adequate living standard, education and other needs are treated as constituting the essential foundation of civil society. A society where there is widespread hunger can only achieve democratic politics very imperfectly. The satisfaction of the basic human need to survive is a necessary platform if democracy is to function. Democratic principles require that each elector or citizen should have an equal voice. To the extent that there is gross inequality in life chances, in access to education for example, the democratic potential of a society is severely limited. At the same time democracy as a collective process is a means whereby such inequalities can be identified and alleviated.

Development and human rights

The same applies to the task of development. Development is only sustainable in the long term if development policies are accountable to the people and are pursued within a framework that respects all human rights and the rule of law. (See question 68.)

59 Are there grounds on which a democratic government can legitimately limit rights?

The international standards permit restriction on the exercise of certain rights on specific grounds, such as public order, public morals, national security and the rights of others. However, certain rights may not be so restricted. Certain fundamental guarantees for the individual, such as freedom from torture, freedom of thought and freedom from discrimination, may never be withdrawn in a democratic society.

Principles governing rights restrictions

The principles concerning the justification of an interference with or restriction of a right are well established in international jurisprudence. These are: that the restriction is provided for by law; that it pursues a legitimate aim, in other words that the purpose of the limitation is clearly one permitted by international standards; and that the necessity for the interference or restriction is made out according to the concept of a democratic society. In practice this means that the government must show that its actions in limiting a right or freedom are proportionate and not excessive.

Exceptional circumstances

Thus, to suppress a political party can never be justified except in the clearest case when an organization has become involved in unconstitutional or violent actions. Equally, it is only in highly exceptional circumstances that international human rights standards would countenance prior censorship of the press. Such an exception might be a newspaper's intention to publish highly sensitive information and the demonstration to a court that publication would put individuals' lives in immediate danger or would threaten the security of the country.

60 Can human rights be suspended in an emergency?

International human rights standards permit the temporary suspension of guarantees of certain civil and political rights in circumstances of a public emergency which 'threatens the life of the nation' and which is officially proclaimed. The most frequently invoked justification by governments for resort to emergency powers is the existence of internal political or ethnic conflict that has developed into violence and terrorism. Typically police or other security forces are given additional powers of arrest and search, and detention without trial may be introduced.

Non-derogable rights

A democratic society will resort to emergency powers with reluctance and implement the principle of exercising special powers to the minimum extent for the shortest period that is necessary and with the maximum safeguards against abuse. Even in an emergency there are certain rights which may not

be suspended (or derogated from), for instance the right to life, freedom of thought and conscience and freedom from torture. These are known as non-derogable rights and are to that extent absolute rights and freedoms.

61 Can a democracy legitimately exclude anyone from citizenship?

The answer is that a state has in principle the right to determine who may become a member or citizen and how citizenship rights are acquired. But in the exercise of this sovereign power it must not behave in a discriminatory way, for example by operating a racially discriminatory immigration policy. It must also abide by any international agreements it has ratified on the admittance of refugees.

Rights of resident aliens

A state may deny political rights to resident non-citizens, although the trend in democratic practice is to offer rights of political participation, including voting rights, to foreign residents following a reasonable period of residence (see question 21). But apart from the political rights that go with citizenship, the state is obliged to ensure that lawfully resident aliens have all other basic rights and freedoms protected without distinction or discrimination.

62 Have minorities any rights in a democracy?

International human rights norms offer specific guarantees for minority communities, whether defined as religious, cultural, national, ethnic or linguistic minorities. Such minorities are entitled not only to have the state recognize their existence, but also to have it protect their specific identity and to encourage conditions for the promotion of that identity. Persons belonging to minorities should have full democratic rights, including the right to participate on equal terms with others in the affairs of the country as well as to participate in decisions that affect their particular communities or the regions in which they live.

UN Declaration on Minorities

These and other principles are set out in the United Nations Declaration on the Rights of Persons Belonging to National or Ethnic, Religious and Linguistic Minorities adopted by the General Assembly of the United Nations in December 1992. Many if not most states have minority communities, and it should be a test of a democratic society that it has a positive approach to the rights of its minorities. Implementing the principles of the new UN Declaration should be a clear and urgent objective for all countries.

63 How are human rights to be defended in practice?

Democratic societies will differ on the means they devise for the protection of rights. However, the international standards offer some guidelines, including the requirement that every individual must have a remedy when a violation of rights is alleged. Individuals should be able to invoke their rights under those international treaties on human rights which their governments have agreed to. All but a few states in the world have written constitutions in which human rights commitments are defined and guaranteed alongside the processes of the democratic system itself. Typically the courts are in the front line in defence of the individual's rights as defined in the constitution's 'Bill of Rights'. Individuals should have unimpeded access to court, including if necessary legal aid, to vindicate their rights. And the decisions and directions of the courts should be implemented by the government; this implementation should include, if the constitution so provides, the rescinding of laws and the payment of compensation. However, the protection of rights also often requires positive action through the adoption of legislative and other measures, to ensure for example the outlawing of all forms of discrimination and the securing of basic entitlements for vulnerable groups, including children, the socially disadvantaged and the disabled.

Institutions for defending rights

In a democracy people often turn to their elected representatives for help in securing justice and their entitlements. The media can equally be of pivotal importance as a watch dog on the abuse of rights. In practice a range of institutions are deployed in the defence of rights, including for example the institution of an ombudsman or independent official to oversee the operation of government administration. But the best defence of democracy is belief in its principles and its purposes. Therefore education at all levels in human rights and democratic citizenship is essential. Education programmes should not be confined to schools and colleges but should extend to public authorities, including such agencies as the police and the military.

5 Democratic or Civil Society

64 What is civil society?

The idea of civil society as a necessary component of democracy is one that has become particularly emphasized as a result of the twentieth-century experience of fascist and communist dictatorships, both of which sought to incorporate and supervise all social institutions under the aegis of the state. The concept of civil society can be looked at from two different aspects: *negatively*, the idea that the reach of the state should be limited, so that it is prevented from controlling all social activity, penetrating all spheres of life, or absorbing all social initiative and talent; *positively*, the idea of having many independent foci of self-organization within society, through which people can work collectively to solve their own problems, which can act as channels of popular opinion and pressure upon government, and which can serve as a protection against its encroachments.

Elements of civil society

Among the chief elements of civil society are: a market economy (see question 9); independent media of communication (question 6); sources of expertise on all aspects of government policy that are independent of the state; above all, a flourishing network of voluntary associations in all areas of social life, through which people manage their own affairs. At different times and places these associations will variously assume a particular significance for the defence and promotion of democracy, whether they be trade unions, professional associations, women's groups, human rights and development organizations, self-help groups, religious bodies or grass-roots organizations of any kind. In an environment of freedom of expression and association such groupings will develop spontaneously, as people recognize the need for collective action to organize their affairs or to defend and advance their interests. They can also be encouraged, however, by public recognition, for example, of their consultative role in relevant areas of government policy.

65   Can civil associations be undemocratic?

The fact that the associations and institutions of civil society are independent, i.e. self-organizing and self-financing, means that they may have the power to modify or even frustrate particular aspects of government policy. The point where this becomes undemocratic is not always easy to define. Most democratically elected governments will consult and compromise with organized social interests, since this is an essential feature of government by consent. However, some interest groups have much more influence over government than others, by virtue of their organization, wealth or connections. Where this influence derives from a mass membership, it must be judged more democratic than where it derives from concentrations of wealth or power in the hands of a few. In addition, associations whose internal organization is itself democratic, such that their leaders can be seen to be genuinely representative of their members, deserve to be treated with greater seriousness than those that are not. Finally, a democratic society ought to acknowledge a special consultative place for organizations representing people who by virtue of social, economic or physical disability have difficulty making their voices heard in the political process, and who would otherwise remain disempowered.

66 Should economic institutions be internally democratic?

Many democrats have argued that the places in which people work are among the most important for determining the character of their lives, and that democratizing the workplace should therefore be a high priority for those seeking a truly democratic society. At a minimum this means preventing any obstruction employers might impose on the self-organization of workers in trade unions, so that they can act collectively to defend or advance their living standards and conditions of work and employment. More ambitious aims include schemes of codetermination and profit-sharing, which give all employees some responsibility for and commitment to the success of an organization as a whole. Although it may be argued that such schemes make it more difficult for employers to dismiss workers, and to ensure labour discipline, there is considerable evidence to suggest that those firms do best in a modern economy which are able to encourage the creative energies of all their employees; and that this is best achieved by treating them as 'citizens' rather than as 'subjects'. Democracy and efficiency, in other words, are not necessarily antithetical, though democratization of the workplace can be expected to generate pressures for moderating large discrepancies in pay and conditions between management and the shop floor.

Accountability of economic institutions

In a democratic society economic institutions also have responsibilities to their local communities, especially for their environmental impact. Just as citizens should have the right of redress against state institutions if their interests are seriously damaged by their activities, so also should they against private firms in the event of assignable damage to their health or physical well-being. Private economic institutions should therefore be expected to operate within an effective framework of legal regulation and environmental protection.

67 Does democracy require private property?

Besides the economic arguments for the institution of private property, in terms of its necessity to a market economy, there are also sound political arguments relating to its importance for sustaining political activity independent of the state. Private property can thus be seen as a central institution of civil society and as a protection for political liberty.

Limits on private property

It does not follow, however, that every state intervention in private property rights should be resisted as a threat to individual freedom. The institution of private property is itself premissed upon a socially recognized and enforced limitation of individual freedom. The exclusive use of any possession presupposes that the freedom of others to have access to it is restricted. The terms on which such freedom is denied must therefore be socially determined and, in principle, be subject to legislative variation as circumstances themselves vary. In short, the use of property may be legitimately controlled by law, and its pattern of distribution may be a legitimate concern of public policy. Although the principle of private property, therefore, is important to democracy, it cannot be a natural or absolute right, but only on terms and within limits that are collectively agreed.

68 Is democracy compatible with economic inequality?

This question cannot be answered with a simple 'yes' or 'no', but is a matter of degree. The greater the economic inequalities in a society, the more difficult it becomes to have effective political equality, since accumulations of wealth can be used as a significant resource to determine political outcomes. In the most extreme cases, the wealthy will see the votes of the poor as a potential threat to their interests, which justifies their manipulating or subverting the electoral process. On the other side, if the poor cannot see any prospect of improving their lot through democratic means, they will not find democracy worth supporting. Here it is not just a question of the quality of democracy, but of its sustainability in any form.

Minimizing political inequality

However, some degree of economic inequality may be both inevitable and justifiable in a market economy. The concern of democrats should be to minimize the political impact or significance of such inequalities as do occur. At one end of the scale there should be strict legislation: limiting the amount of money that can be spent on election campaigns by both parties and individual candidates; preventing concentrations of media ownership; and requiring the disclosure of sources of funding for parties and public campaigning of all kinds.

111

At the other end of the scale all citizens should be guaranteed those minimum necessities of life that are the condition for the exercise of any effective citizenship.

69 Does democracy depend upon economic development?

There is considerable evidence that the prospects for sustaining democracy, without slipping back into authoritarian rule, are greater the more economically developed a country is. This is because of the effects that economic development has upon the character of the citizen body and the structure of civil society. With widespread literacy and education comes a more mature and informed electorate. With an expanded middle class, performing a variety of technical and professional roles, there is greater resistance to paternalistic or authoritarian forms of government. And the process of economic development enhances the complexity of civil society and the variety of self-organizing groups and associations with the confidence to defend their independence against government encroachment.

Exceptions

It would be wrong, however, to conclude that democracy can only be sustained where there is a high level of economic development. There are examples of countries in all continents that have maintained open electoral competition and civil and political liberties over decades despite low levels of economic development as measured by per capita GNP (e.g. India, Jamaica, Botswana). Government policies to encourage universal literacy may be more important than the particular level of economic development. And what fledgling democracies need more than anything else is *sustainable* economic growth, from whatever level of development they start, so

113

that different sections of society are able to share in improvement, and the intensity of distributional conflicts is moderated. The policies of the principal international economic agencies, and of developed countries, can be a significant help or hindrance in this context.

70 Does religion help or hinder democracy?

This is another question to which there is no simple 'yes' or 'no' answer, since so much depends upon the context. It is not even possible to separate the great world faiths into hard and fast categories, such as those which are supportive of democracy, those which are neutral, and those whose effects are disabling to it, since all religions contain within them a variety of competing tendencies. Historically, Christianity supported both the divine right of kings and egalitarian republicanism. At one and the same time influential groups within this and other faiths have worked to support authoritarian regimes, while others have risked their lives to protect opponents of them, or to expose their human rights violations.

Religion and the state

It can be argued that a hierarchically ordered religion, in which believers accept without question the truths that are handed down from above, will be less conducive to the democratic spirit than one whose matters of belief are subject to lively debate and interpretation among the faithful. More crucial for democracy than the question of internal organization, however, is the relation of a given religion to the state. The closer the link between them, the less likely it is that those who belong to a different faith will be treated as equal citizens. In the extreme case, where the religious authorities

114

regard the state as the divine instrument for fulfilling a religious mission on earth, politics can readily take on the character of a crusade in which members of other faiths are forced into line and persecuted and all freedom of expression becomes stifled.

Religious toleration

It has been from the painful historical experience of such oppressions, and of the civil wars and communal violence they have generated, that the idea of religious toleration has emerged. Even if we believe our religion to possess the final and exclusive truth, the cost of compelling others to accept it is simply too high in human terms to be sustainable in a world characterized by a pluralism of different faiths. Toleration does not mean abandoning our own convictions, or refraining from proselytizing others; it means according people the basic human dignity of letting them decide for themselves, even when that leads them to decide wrongly.

Minority religions

The most effective environment in which both tolerance and acceptance of diversity of religion or belief can be secured is one in which no religious faith is given a privileged position within the state. Such a state may act to support religious faiths in an even-handed way, through taxation or assistance for religious schooling. Toleration may even persist in a state that involves one religion in matters, say, of state ceremonial, where it forms the religion of the large majority. However, once the state seeks to impose the precepts of a majority religion on non-believers, it will inevitably come to abrogate the basic democratic freedoms of expression and association of those who dissent, including those within the majority religion itself. Here we may note the divergence between what the majority at a given moment may want and what the conditions for the ongoing popular control of government and for political equality may require.

71 Is democracy possible where religious or ethnic conflicts exist?

It is difficult to dispute the conclusion that without some sense of common political identity among the people of a given territory free institutions are difficult to sustain. This identity may be derived from a shared historical experience which transcends the differences of religion, ethnicity, language or whatever. It may also be fostered by political institutions that are recognized as treating all groups fairly, and to which they have all freely consented. Nothing fuels communal antagonism more surely than when exclusion from political office brings with it the experience of discrimination, disadvantage or oppression for one or other community, or the fear that it will do so. Short-sighted political leaders may gain temporary advantage by playing on such fears. However, secessions or partition, even when they are practicable, tend to be desperate remedies, which may simply transfer the problem to a different point, by creating a newly aggrieved minority. It is no answer to historical oppression to construct new oppressions for the future.

Constitutional safeguards

Given the intermingling of different peoples, races and faiths which is the norm for contemporary societies, all require constitutional arrangements that serve to protect minorities against systematic discrimination and oppression (see questions 10, 12, 50 and 63). No newly created state should be accorded international recognition until it has shown convincing evidence that such arrangements are in place.

72 In what ways is the institution of the family relevant to democracy?

Historically, and in most societies still today, families have tended to be organized in such a way that women undertake the major responsibility for child-rearing and child-care, for looking after the home and for servicing the domestic needs

of men. These domestic arrangements, which appear to be an essentially private matter, have an important public significance: in limiting the time and energy women have available for public activities, and in defining the kinds of public role that are deemed suitable for them to fulfil. To the extent that these arrangements and the attitudes supporting them persist, women will be denied equality of political opportunity, and the quality of democratic life will suffer through their absence. The public status of women can be enhanced, however, by appropriate government policies, and through the influence exerted by women themselves, via woman's organizations, self-help groups, etc. (see question 26).

Children and democracy

The family also has a public significance in the positive role it can play in assisting the development of future citizens. The childhood experiences of being valued equally, of learning both to have a say in domestic affairs and to respect the voices of others, of understanding that the exercise of rights entails corresponding duties – these are learning processes that are important for the later exercise of democratic citizenship. It is also through the family that children first learn attitudes towards the wider community and develop opinions about political affairs that may persist through their adult lives.

73 What role can schools play in education for democracy?

Besides the development of particular skills and capacities, especially literacy and the transmission of knowledge, schools play a significant part in the handing on of a society's cultures and traditions. They also have a role in the critical evaluation

of those cultures, and in helping children understand their place in an interdependent world of many faiths and beliefs. More specific training for democracy will lead to an understanding of the country's constitution and how it came to be developed; a practical knowledge of the rights and duties of citizenship; and an appreciation of human rights and their importance. A democratic education involves not only the acquisition of knowledge, however. It is also fostered through the experiences of debate on issues of current importance, of presenting arguments and listening to the views of others, and of sharing in collective decisions on matters

119

affecting the life of the school and its community, for example through classroom assemblies, elected school councils, and so on. The ages appropriate for the acquisition of these different skills and areas of knowledge will obviously differ according to the country and the pattern of its education system. For a democracy to overlook them, however, for example because they are too 'political', would be to incur the risk of serious erosion of its popular base.

74 How can a culture of democracy be fostered?

Democratic thinkers have always argued that the practice of working democratic institutions helps develop a democratic culture, for example through the incentive it gives people to become informed about the issues on which they will have to decide, and through the skills and attitudes fostered by political participation at every level. The opportunities for such participation, therefore, both in the formal political sphere and in the associations and institutions of civil society, should be as widespread as possible. These institutions, including political parties and voluntary associations of all kinds, can themselves be a significant resource for the political education of their members.

Fostering a democratic culture

A democratic culture is also fostered in many other ways, besides the schooling mentioned in question 73. The arts can be an important vehicle for democratic ideas and practice, for the reflective articulation of contemporary problems and discontents and for the representation of a society to itself. Public ceremonial can be used to celebrate specifically democratic and popular aspects of a country's history and its institutions. Above all, the media play a crucial role in political education in the widest sense: in enhancing the level of public information and awareness, in the critical assessment of government policy and in providing a channel through which members of the public can communicate with one another.

6 The Future of Democracy

75 What are the main problems facing democracy today?

The most acute problems facing democracy today are those deriving from the economic sphere, which currently affects the populations of most countries of the world. The developed economies are experiencing levels of persistent unemployment unknown since the 1930s, with correspondingly worrying implications for state budgets and welfare provision. Countries that have emerged from a Communist past are undergoing the shocks of privatization and marketization of their economies, which bring widespread insecurity, intensified inequality and the danger of hyperinflation. Many less developed countries have endured zero- or minusgrowth for years, with its attendant impoverishment of the population, cuts in welfare programmes and the threat of famine.

Economic hardship

The experience of economic hardship on the scale currently afflicting so many countries and peoples has inevitable political consequences. It intensifies social antagonisms of all kinds, by making the struggle for economic opportunities more intense and the cost of losing out more insupportable. It encourages economic migration, which in turn generates hostility to immigrants and demands for a fortress state among the more developed countries. Conditions of economic depression make it much more difficult to realize the ideal of equal citizenship, and lead to a loss of confidence in the capacity of democratic government to provide solutions to society's problems. While robust democratic systems may be able to withstand these shocks, they are much more damaging to fledgling democracies, which need relatively favourable circumstances in which to become securely established.

Loss of political control

Three features of the current economic depression have particularly served to undermine confidence in democratic governments. The first is that many of the processes and institutions which determine the economic fortunes of a country now lie outside its borders, and hence beyond the control of the supposedly sovereign state. This loss of economic control affects all countries, but especially the less developed; they can do little to influence the prices of raw materials or the terms of debt repayment and inward investment, which matter so much to them. This situation has been exacerbated, secondly, by the prevailing economic orthodoxy of the past two decades, which has held that governments can do little to fashion or improve their countries' economic destinies, which are determined by market forces and by the responses of individuals and firms to the opportunities of the market. Accompanying this belief has been, thirdly, a powerful ethos of individual and familial self-interest, which has undermined the sense of collective responsibility that might sustain a more active government, or a more generous spirit to those less fortunately placed, whether at home or abroad. The idea that the problems of economic and social interdependence require collective solutions still awaits a convincing rearticulation in a world in which socialism has become discredited and any progressive internationalism is at a discount.

76 Can poor societies really afford democracy?

The idea that poor societies cannot afford democracy embraces a number of rather different concerns. One is that the organization of democracy is expensive and time-consuming, and that a state's scarce resources of time and money would be better spent on more urgent needs of its population, such as health, education and helping ensure basic economic survival. In comparison with these, the organization of elections, the training of officials for democratic roles, the delays in policy formation and execution necessitated by parliamentary and public accountability, and so on, seem an unaffordable luxury.

Disadvantages of democracy

To this narrowly financial argument can be added a broader concern to the effect that the disadvantages of democracy may far outweigh its advantages in societies with developing economies and governmental systems. The social and political divisiveness of electoral competition is especially damaging where states themselves are recently established and national identity is barely developed. Moreover, the informed and mature electorate that is needed if democracy is not to degenerate into short-termism, demagogy or outright intolerance is typically the product of economic development. It is not just that national unity and economic development are more urgent national priorities than democracy, from this point of view; in the historical order of things they have to be established *before* democracy, for which they provide the necessary platform or prerequisite.

Democracy and development

Particular features of these objections and difficulties have been dealt with in the answers to earlier questions (e.g. 13, 36, 69), but it will be useful to bring them together. To begin with, economic development cannot be treated as a purely quantitative concept to be measured, say, by GNP per head of population. It is also a qualitative concept, about the well-being of a population, to which considerations of income distribution and the distribution of state expenditure (as between health or education and the armed forces) are particularly relevant. Now it so happens that these qualitative aspects of economic development are themselves dependent upon the character of a political regime and the degree of its responsiveness to the population. Democratic electorates are more likely to demand policies that moderate the extremes of economic inequality, and to support state spending on health, education and the physical infrastructure rather than on the military or on prestige projects with little social utility. Moreover, an open and accountable regime will use public resources more efficiently than a closed or authoritarian one. It will also be one in which major scandals, such as widespread human rights abuses, environmental degradation or famine, cannot survive undetected for years. The positive relation between democracy, development and the protection of human rights was underlined in the Final Document of the Vienna World Conference on Human Rights in June 1993.

Improving democracies

The issue should therefore be whether a society can afford *not* to have a democracy, given the depths to which unaccountable and unresponsive political power can sink. It should also be how to enable democracies to work better, and in a way that matches the particular circumstances and requirements

125

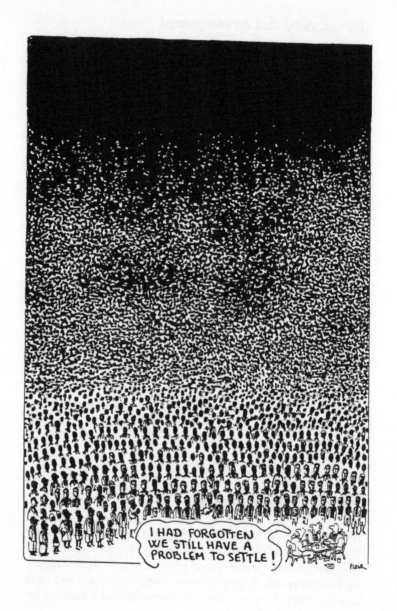

of the countries concerned, rather than give up on them altogether.

77 What can developed democracies do to help developing ones?

Developed democracies can do a lot to assist developing ones. At the most general level they can give whole-hearted recognition to the right to development and the consequential duties of the international community towards developing countries. More specifically, they can assist them by offering training and disseminating good democratic practice. Developing democracies can be helped with the training of all kinds of public officials: election officers, parliamentary clerks, constitutional lawyers, financial controllers, members of the legislature, party officials, and so on. The dissemination of good practice is most fully developed in the fields of electoral competition, where international panels are a widely accepted device for assessing how far elections are free and fair, and of human rights, where clear international standards exist for both the content and the procedures of human rights provisions. However, the establishment of standards of good practice could be extended to many other areas of the democratic process, including open and accountable government. In all these areas the performance of some developed democracies may themselves leave a good deal to be desired; and their assistance to others will be the more credible the more they show themselves ready to improve their own processes to the level of the best international practice.

Sovereignty and international intervention

More controversial than assistance in these aspects of democratization is the contemporary practice of using economic development aid, and the threat of withholding it, as a lever

127

to accelerate multi-party elections or to enforce compliance with minimum human rights standards (so-called 'political conditionality'). Those who support such policies of the developed world argue that for too long development aid has been used to sustain authoritarian regimes with records of human rights abuses, and that 'conditionality' will encourage opposition groups and those campaigning for democracy within the country concerned. Those opposed to the policy argue that it is inconsistent in operation, because it is subordinated to other foreign policy goals, that it is uncertain in its effects, because it encourages merely token compliance, and that there is something contradictory about seeking to promote internal self-determination by means of external compulsion. Much depends upon the particular context and manner of such policies. What is undoubted is that we are increasingly moving into a world where considerations of 'sovereignty' are no longer acceptable to protect states from external pressure when they seriously abuse their own citizens (see question 55). Yet such pressure is more effectively exerted through the enforcement of accepted human rights conventions by established regional or international bodies than by bilateral donors.

Democracy and 'structural adjustment'

A different objection to policies of political conditionality on the part of the developed world is directed not to the policies as such, but to the contradiction of supporting democracy with one hand while pursuing economic policies of structural adjustment and debt repayment with the other, which may play their part in weakening fragile democracies still further. The benefit of economic aid can be simply overwhelmed by the demands of interest repayment on foreign debt. And the requirements of 'structural adjustment' can, through the indiscriminate reduction of public expenditure, threaten those programmes on which the poor of a country rely, and which are most important in sustaining public support for the

democratic process and in generating confidence that their government is in control of its own economic destiny.

78 Can international institutions be democratized?

One of the main problems facing contemporary democracies is the erosion of self-determination, because so much of what affects the well-being of their populations now lies beyond national control. The economic dimension of this erosion of national autonomy has been discussed in previous questions (75 and 77). The problem extends, however, to a wide range of issues, including environmental degradation, control over natural resources, population movements, as well as the more traditional military threats. No society today can insulate itself from the effects of what happens beyond its borders.

Forms of accountability

The urgent questions for democracy therefore are, first, how to create or consolidate those international institutions that can act to regulate and control the global forces and trans-national private corporations which shape the destiny of nations; second, how to subject these institutions to meaning-ful democratic accountability. Many such institutions already exist at both regional and global level in the form of intergov-ernmental treaties, and there are institutions of a more general scope and permanency such as the IMF, the International Court and the UN itself. The limitation of such bodies from a democratic point of view is that they mostly operate according to a narrowly intergovernmental model of repres-entation and accountability: are responsive to governments rather than to a cross-national public opinion; have limited powers of enforcement over intransigent member states; and

are mostly weighted according to past imperial status or
current power, rather than according to population.

World parliament

Progress towards the democratization of international institutions is likely to be slow and to take the form of extending
the reach of existing bodies, such as human rights conventions and courts or regional parliaments like the European
Parliament. The urgency of the need for international solutions to global problems, however, makes the aim of a world
parliament with effective enforcement powers, and a corresponding conception of world citizenship, neither Utopian
nor fanciful.

79 Will national identities become submerged by the new 'global society'?

It is a paradoxical feature of the recent processes of 'global-
ization' that they provoke the assertion of local identities and
historical cultures at the same time that they link the destinies
of the world's peoples more closely together. There is little
danger that the distinctiveness of national cultures and traditions will disappear. Indeed, a certain security of national
identity could be seen as a precondition of a more confident
and generous internationalism. What is likely in the future is
that the monopoly of the nation-state in constituting the only
legitimate source of political allegiance for its citizens will
give way to a more pluralistic and multiple set of political
identities. People will come to define themselves as members
of a locality, of a nation or multi-national federation, or a
region or sub-continent, and as citizens of the world. Such a
development should be welcomed by democrats, since the
universalizing thrust of democracy and its principles points
its adherents beyond the confines of the nation-state and

131

beyond any exclusive commitment to one single level of political allegiance.

80 How can democracy be made relevant to ordinary people?

It is appropriate to end a book of questions and answers on democracy with this most crucial question of all. If ordinary people see no point in democracy, because it seems to have no relevance to their everyday lives and the situations in which they live them, they will not do anything to defend it. If the choices they are offered at election time make no difference to them, because politicians lack the power or the will to change anything in the direction people have voted for; if the basic civil and political rights are not sufficiently guaranteed to enable people to organize and campaign on public issues without fear; above all, if people have no power to affect their situations at the most local level of the workplace and the neighbourhood – then democracy has become an empty shell, a form without any substance. The task facing democrats everywhere is how to strengthen the substance behind the form, how to make the principles of popular control and political equality more institutionally effective, whether it be in the democratization of a previously authoritarian regime or in the renewal and deepening of democracies that are longer established.

Further Reading

Arblaster, Anthony, 1994. *Democracy*, Buckingham: Open University Press, 2nd edition.

Bobbio, Norberto, 1987. *The Future of Democracy*, Cambridge: Polity Press.

Dahl, Robert, 1989. *Democracy and its Critics*, New Haven and London: Yale University Press.

Dunn, John ed., 1992. *Democracy: the Unfinished Journey*, Oxford: Oxford University Press.

Hadenius, Axel, 1992. *Democracy and Development*, Cambridge: Cambridge University Press.

Hannum, Hurst, 1990. *Autonomy, Sovereignty and Self-Determination*, Philadelphia: University of Pennsylvania Press.

Held, David ed., 1993. *Prospects for Democracy*, Cambridge: Polity Press.

Huntington, Samuel, 1991. *The Third Wave: Democratization in the Late Twentieth Century*, Norman and London: University of Oklahoma Press.

Keane, John, 1991. *The Media and Democracy*, Cambridge: Polity Press.

Lijphart, Arend, 1984. *Democracies*, New Haven and London: Yale University Press.

Nickel, James W., 1987. *Making Sense of Human Rights*, Berkeley: University of California Press.

Plattner, Marc and Diamond, Larry eds, 1992. *Capitalism, Socialism and Democracy* (Journal of Democracy special issue no. 3.3), Baltimore: Johns Hopkins University Press.

Rodley, Nigel, 1987. *The Treatment of Prisoners under International Law*, Oxford: Oxford University Press.

Rosas, Allan and Helgesen, Jan eds, 1992. *Human Rights and Pluralist Democracy*, Dordrecht: Martinus Nijhoff.

United Nations, 1988–. *Human Rights Fact Sheet Series.*

United Nations, 1993. *Human Rights: a Compilation of International Instruments*, two volumes.